The rules and regulations, with an alphabetical list of the members of the army and Navy Club – Primary Source Edition

Army and Navy Club, London

THE

RULES AND REGULATIONS,

WITH

AN ALPHABETICAL LIST

OF

THE MEMBERS

OF THE

ARMY AND NAVY CLUB.

LONDON:

H. M. POLLETT, 35 & 36, ALDERMANBURY.

1861.

7924
17|III|90

ARMY AND NAVY CLUB.

PRESIDENT.

GENERAL COMMANDING-IN-CHIEF.
HIS ROYAL HIGHNESS
GEORGE DUKE OF CAMBRIDGE,
K.G., K.P., G.C.B., G.C.M.G.,
&c., &c., &c.

TRUSTEES.

GENERAL SIR JAMES WATSON. K.C.B.
GENERAL THOMAS JOHN FORBES, Royal Artillery.
CAPTAIN THOMAS PORTER, Royal Navy.

COMMITTEE OF MANAGEMENT.
1860-61.

1. ALVES, JOHN, Major-General, ret. full pay
3. BLANE, GEORGE, Commander Royal Navy
2. BOGGIS, J. E., Captain H.P. 55th Regiment
1. BRYSON, ALEX., *M.D.*, Inspector of Hospitals and Fleets
1. CHICHESTER, Lord·JOHN, late Captain 87th Fusiliers
1. CLARKE, J., WALROND, late Captain 10th Hussars
1. COWLEY, Norman, late Lieutenant 5th Dragoon Guards
2. DANIELL, HENRY, Colonel, late Coldstream Guards
1. GALLWEY, HENRY J., Commander Royal Navy
2. GARVAGH, C. H., Lord, late Captain 7th Hussars
1. GRANT, W. L., late Captain 7th Fusiliers
1. HAWKINS, FRANK K., Commander Royal Navy
3. HAY, DAVID, Lieut.-Colonel, late 6th Dragoon Guards
2. JEFFERSON, RICHARD, Lieut. H. P. Ceylon Rifle Regt
3. KEANE, Hon. HUSSEY F., Major Royal Engineers
3. KERIN, F. G., Surgeon 2nd Life Guards
2. LINDOW, H. W., late Lieutenant 17th Lancers
2. MURRAY, Hon. HENRY A., Captain Royal Navy
1. OTWAY, ARTHUR J., late Lieutenant 2nd Regiment
1. PEARSON, R. L. O., Major Grenadier Guards
3. REYNOLDS, C. W., late Captain 16th Lancers
1. ST. LEGER, J., Major, late 14th Light Dragoons
1. SURTEES, H. E., late Lieutenant 10th Hussars
2. YONGE, WILLIAM L., Captain Royal Artillery

Bankers.—UNION BANK OF LONDON, 4, Pall Mall East
Solicitor.—G. BENTINCK LEFROY, Esq., 5, Robert Street, Adelphi
Secretary.—THOMAS WALCOT, Esq.

*** By the figures 1, 2, 3, it is shown whether the Member is in his first, second, or third year of Management.

INDEX TO THE RULES AND REGULATIONS.

RULES AND REGULATIONS

OF THE

ARMY AND NAVY CLUB.

THE Army and Navy Club is instituted for the association of Commissioned Officers of all Ranks in Her Majesty's Regular Army, Royal Navy, and Royal Marines; and shall not exceed 1800 effective Members, independent of those returned from Supernumerary List; after which ballots will only take place as vacancies occur in the Effective List from Death and Retirements.

Design

I.—The Members shall consist of all Officers in the Regular Army, including the Medical and Commissariat Staff; the Royal Navy, Physicians and Surgeons thereof; the Royal Marines, and Marine Artillery Corps; who are on full-pay, retired pay, or half-pay, at the date of their entry in the Candidates' book, and holding Commissions from Her Majesty, or from the Lords of the Admiralty; and Midshipmen who have attained the age of 17 years, and are in the Service at the date of their ballot: any Officer who has retired from the Service, but allowed to retain his rank.

Who are eligible to become Members

B

Honorary
Members.

II.—Princes of the Blood Royal, and also the following Members of Her Majesty's Government, whilst holding Office :—The principal Secretaries of State for the War and Colonial Departments, the Paymaster-General of the Army and Navy, and the Judge Advocates-General of the Army and Navy—shall be eligible to become Honorary Members ; but if any of the Principals of those Departments shall be otherwise eligible, they shall not be Honorary, but may become Supernumerary Members, without ballot, upon paying the entrance and annual subscriptions, until vacancies occur to make them effective Members. The Commander-in-chief, the Master-General, of the Ordnance, the Adjutant-General, the Quarter-Master-General, the Military Secretary, to the Commander-in-chief of Her Majesty's Forces, the Lords of the Admiralty, and the Secretary of the Admiralty for the time being not being Members, and being otherwise eligible than by virtue of their respective offices, may become Supernumerary Members without ballot, upon paying the entrance and annual subscriptions, till vacancies occur to make them effective Members.

The Committee of Management shall have the power of inviting the foregoing to become Honorary or Supernumerary Members ; and also Foreigners

of distinguished rank, or British Subjects holding
rank as Military or Naval Officers in the Service of
Foreign Powers, as Honorary Visitors, *temporarily
visiting England*, during such visit.

Charles Downes, ·Esq., having had so great a
share in the Establishment of the Club, and having
been appointed Treasurer, shall be an Honorary
Member, and continue as such, notwithstanding he
should relinquish the office of Treasurer; in which
case it shall be for the consideration of the Club
whether the future Treasurer shall be an Honorary
Member.

The Secretary, whilst holding office, shall be an
Honorary Member, but shall not have any vote in
the management of the proceedings of the Club.

III.—Any Member who shall be cashiered or
dismissed the Service, or who shall retire from the
Service to avoid a Court Martial, or who shall be
convicted in a Civil Court of any Criminal offence,
shall, *ipso facto*, cease to be a Member of the Club;
should it however be the opinion of any fifty Members (not being of the Committee) that the cause
of his quitting the Service does not affect his character as a gentleman, or should the criminal conviction
be from subsequent evidence set aside, he shall be

Who are liable to be discontinued as Members.

eligible for re-election, without payment of entrance fee. A list of the fifty Members writing for his re-instatement must be forwarded to the Committee, who shall then cause his name to be placed as a Candidate for re-admission in the public room during fourteen days, at the expiration of which time he shall be balloted for from 12 to 4 o'clock, p.m., according to Rule VII. Sixty Members shall be required to make the ballot valid, and two-thirds of the Members voting shall be requisite for his re-admission.

If any Member shall be made a Bankrupt, or seek to obtain his discharge from his debts under the Insolvent Debtors' Act, he shall, *ipso facto*, cease to be a Member of the Club; but upon application being made by him to the Committee, stating the cause of his Bankruptcy or Insolvency, such person may be re-admitted by the Committee (who shall be specially summoned for that purpose,) if a majority of two-thirds of such Committee be of opinion that his character as a gentleman is not affected thereby. But in the event of a majority only being in favor of his re-admission, then the name of such person shall be put up for re-admission by ballot, free of all entrance fees.

Any Officer on half-pay who shall have retired

from full-pay in consequence of any regimental Who are in eligible to be come Mem- bers.
proceeding affecting his character as a gentleman,
shall not be eligible to become a Member.

IV.—In case the conduct of any Member, either Persons lia ble to be dis continued as Members.
in or out of the Club-house, shall in the opinion of
the Committee, or of any fifty Members of the
Club, who shall certify the same to them in writing,
be injurious to the character and interests of the
Club, the Committee shall be empowered to recommend such Member to resign; and if the
Member so recommended shall not do so within
a month from the date of the letter of such recommendation, the Committee shall then call a General
Meeting of the Members, and if a majority of
two-thirds of that meeting agree to the expulsion
of such Member, his name shall be erased from
the list, and be for ever afterwards ineligible for
re-election, except under circumstances set forth
in the preceding Rule: provided that no such
recommendation be sent to any Member unless
the resolution to send the same shall have been
agreed to by two-thirds of the Members of the
Committee actually present, all of whom to have
been specially summoned for that purpose. Provided also that if on the Meeting of the Committee
specially summoned, they unanimously are of opinion

that the offence of a Member is sufficient for the interests of the Club to warrant his immediate expulsion, they be empowered to suspend from such Member the use and advantages of the Club until an Extraordinary Meeting can be held, which Meeting must be convened within twenty-one days after the suspension. Whenever a General Meeting is summoned to consider the re-admission of a Member, the ballot shall take place at once if the proposal be entertained, and be kept open for two hours after the Meeting has terminated.

Members retiring from the Service. V.—Members retiring from their respective services shall not be thereby ineligible to continue Members, unless as provided for by Rule IV.

Candidates. VI.—Candidates must be proposed by one Member, and seconded by another. The Candidate's name, rank, service, and station, or residence, shall be inserted, at the time of his being proposed, in the Candidate-book, at least one month previously to the day of ballot. The Proposer and Seconder are held responsible for the eligibility of the Candidate, agreeably to the rules of the Club.

VII.—The admission of Members into the Club shall be by ballot, excepting as provided for in Rule II.; and the names of Candidates, when balloted for, shall be taken in regular succession as to seniority on the list.

VIII.—The Ballot (when there are vacancies) Ballot. may take place on the 5th of each month, except that day should happen to fall on a Sunday, and then on the following day, from 12 to 4 o'clock; three Members of the Committee and the Secretary shall open the boxes and declare the result. No ballot shall be valid unless thirty Members actually vote; and one black ball in ten to exclude. No Candidate who shall have been twice rejected, shall be eligible to be proposed again.

The list of the Candidates, with the names of the Proposer and Seconder, shall be placed in a conspicuous part of the Club-room fourteen days previous to the ballot.

No Member shall be allowed to ballot for a Candidate, or to vote on any occasion whatever, until all his subscriptions are paid agreeably to the rules.

IX.—ENTRANCE—The Entrance Subscription on Subscrip Admission shall be Thirty Pounds. tions.

ANNUAL.—The Annual Subscription shall be six Guineas, payable in advance on the 1st of January in each year; and an Annual Subscription of Five Shillings from each Member, for a Library, payable at the same time.

X.—Every new Member is expected to pay his subscription on receiving the official notification of his election; and if the subscription of such new Member be not paid within two months, if in the United Kingdom; four months in Europe or America; eight months in all other places; the Secretary shall report accordingly to the Committee for the time being, who shall cause his name to be erased from the books of the Club, unless the Member can justify the delay to the satisfaction of the Committee.

XI.—All Subscriptions shall be paid into the Union Bank of London, 4, Pall Mall East, to the account of the Trustees.

XII.—No newly-elected or Supernumerary Member shall participate in any of the advantages or privileges of the Club until all his subscriptions are paid agreeably to the Rules.

XIII.—The name of every Member failing to pay his Annual Subscription, due on the 1st of January, shall be placed in the Club-room on the 1st of February, and notified by the Secretary to him, his agent, or banker, provided the addresses of either are known to the Secretary; and if the subscription be not paid on or before the 1st of March, the defaulter shall cease to be a Member, his name be erased from the books, and an effective Member elected at the next ballot. Any Member, however, who shall have been in the Club-house during January, and not have paid his subscription on or before the last day of that month, or who shall use the Club after the 1st of February without having paid his subscription shall without further notice, cease to be a Member of the Club. But if the Member assign to the Committee reasons for the omission, which they shall deem satisfactory, the Committee shall re-admit him upon the payment of the arrears, and a fine of £5, if the Member shall have been in the Club-house since the 1st of January; and £2 should he not have been in the House.

To avoid inconvenience, all Members liable to the Annual Subscriptions are earnestly requested to furnish their agents or bankers with a general authority to pay the same when due.

XIV.—Members proceeding abroad on duty, whether on civil, military, or naval service, may, on their application to the Committee, become Supernumerary Members, and be exempt from the payment of their Annual Subscriptions, with the exception of that for the Library, commencing

Exemptions from Annual Subscriptions.

from the 1st of January following their Departure from the United Kingdom; and Members who are on foreign service when elected, whether civil, military, or naval, shall likewise be exempt from the Annual Subscriptions, with the exception of that for the Library, until their return to the United Kingdom.

Members ordered on foreign service, and embarking on or before the 31st of January, if their Subscriptions have been paid for both the previous and current years, will upon application to the Committee, be placed on the Supernumerary list, and have the Annual Subscription for the current year returned to them, and will be further entitled to enjoy all the privileges of the Club for the said month, provided always that the above-named application be lodged with the Secretary on or before the 31st of January.

But Members elected, and Supernumerary Members, not having received the advantages of the foregoing clause, and returning from foreign service between the 1st of October and the 31st of December in each year, are not to pay the Annual Subscription for the current year, but to enjoy all the privileges of the Club, and the Annual Subscription to commence on the 1st of January following.

Members proceeding abroad, otherwise than on public duty, may also, on their application to the Committee, be placed on the Supernumerary List, and be exempt from the payment of their Annual Subscriptions, with the exception of that for the Library, provided they continue absent from the United Kingdom for one year, commencing from the 1st January after their departure. In such case it shall, however, be necessary that the Member shall report his intention to be absent from the United Kingdom, and obtain the sanction of the Committee, prior to his being placed on the Supernumerary List.

In all instances of Members returning from abroad, the date of their return must be officially reported to the Secretary, and the Annual Subscription for the current year paid within two months after their return, or such Member will be considered as having resigned, unless the cause for such notification or payment not having been made within the period prescribed be deemed satisfactory to the Committee.

The non-payment of the Library Subscription for two years shall be considered as a resignation, and the Member cease to belong to the Club. But if he assigns reasons for the omission, which are deemed satisfactory by the Committee, they shall re-admit him upon payment of the arrears.

Members withdrawing from the Club. XV.—Any Member intending to withdraw from the Club shall signify his intention so to do in writing to the Secretary, before the 1st of January, otherwise his name shall be placed up in the Club-room on the 1st of February, and be subject to the provisions of the 13th Rule.

Members discontinuing as such, not to have any claim on the Club Any Member who shall cease to belong to the Club, either by resignation or otherwise, shall have no claim upon, or be entitled to participate in, any of the effects or property belonging to the Club, nor to have any part of his Annual Subscription for the current year returned.

Vacancies. XVI.—Vacancies of Members becoming Supernumerary, or otherwise, shall be filled up by ballot; and Supernumerary Members on their return to England, and paying the Annual Subscriptions, as required, shall be entitled to all the privileges of the Club, and become effective Members as vacancies occur.

Committee. XVII.—All the concerns of the Club, the providing by agreement, lease, or by building, a suitable house, if approved of by a General Meeting, the domestic and other arrangements and regulations for its establishment and management, shall be conducted by a Committee, consisting of twenty-four Members. The Trustees, if not already Members, shall be ex-officio Members, but shall not be entitled to vote in the Committee upon questions relating to the investiture of the funds in Government or other securities, or the sale thereof, previously to the appropriation of such funds to the permanent use of the Club.

The present authorised appropriation of the rooms of the Club-house shall not be altered, except by a resolution passed at an Annual General Meeting, notice of such proposed alteration being duly given. This resolution is not to apply to any temporary appropriation of rooms during the time the House is under repair.

XVIII.—The Committee shall be elected at the Annual General Meeting, to be held on the Monday in the Derby week. Every Member shall retire at the third General Meeting after his election, as also every Member who has failed to attend the General Committee twelve times previous to the Candidates' Book being placed on the table. This book shall be placed in the Morning-room at least two months previous to the Annual Meeting, wherein any Member may put the names of any Members up to twelve, who he may recommend to fill the vacancies in the Committee; and, to prevent unnecessary confusion, a printed list of the Committee shall be placed on the first page of this book, with a pen mark drawn through the names of those Members who retire according to the foregoing paragraph. The list to be closed three clear days previous to the General Meeting, for the purpose of examination by the Committee, and the Members who have the greatest number of votes shall fill the vacancies in rotation; any vacancy occuring during the year shall also be filled up from the same list by the Member having the next greatest number of votes; but no Member shall be added to the Committee from the aforesaid list, beyond the first twelve. Should a vacancy occur in the Committee after the twelve numbers have been filled up, the Candidate Book shall be laid upon the table for election during one month.

Meetings of Committee.
XIX.—The Committee shall hold an ordinary meeting in every week, or oftener if required, to transact the current business, and to audit the accounts. Three shall form a quorum. The day of

meeting to be announced by a notice affixed in the dining-room.

XX.—There shall be three Trustees, in whose names, under the direction of the Committee, all securities shall be taken and investments made; the whole property of the Club being, notwithstanding, subject to the disposition of the Committee, and their order in writing, signed by the Chairman, with two other Members, countersigned by the Secretary, shall be obligatory upon, and full authority for, the Trustees; and if any Trustee declines to act, or is rendered ineligible as a Trustee, by going abroad, or otherwise, he shall be replaced by another, to be named by the Committee; such nomination to be subject to the approval of the next General Meeting. *Trustees.*

XXI.—Treasurers shall be appointed by the Committee, subject to the approval of the next General Meeting following the appointment, who shall make a report to them, when required, of all payments and receipts. *Treasurer.*

XXII.—The Accounts of the Club to be in future audited by a Public Accountant, to be selected by the Committee. *Auditors.*

Secretary
and
Vacancies

XXIII.—Any vacancies occasioned by death or resignation of Trustee, Treasurer, or Secretary, shall be filled up by the Committee, when not less than seven Members are present, subject to the approval of the next General Meeting following the appointment.

Accounts

XXIV.—A report and abstract of the Accounts and general concerns of the Club, up to the 31st of December previous, signed by the Public Accountant, together with an estimate of the probable receipts and expenditure for the current year, signed by the Chairman of the Committee, shall be submitted to the Annual General Meeting on Monday in the Derby week, and printed for the use of the Members.

Payment of
Funds

XXV.—All payments, under the authority of the Trustees, to be made upon the orders of the Committee, signed by the Chairman, with two other Members, and countersigned by the Secretary.

Annual
General
Meeting.

XXVI.—There shall be an Annual General Meeting of the Members held on Monday in the Derby week, for the purpose of receiving from the Committee a report of the general concerns of the Club, electing Auditors and new Members for the Committee, and discussing all proposals which may require the decision of a General Meeting : a majority of the Members present at such Meeting shall decide. The chair to be taken at all General Meetings at two o'clock, and one of the Trustees or a Member of the Committee to preside.

XXVII.—The Committee may call an Extra-ordinary General Meeting of the Club, on giving fourteen days' notice, *specifying the object in the form of a Resolution, and confining the discussion to that object only*, providing always that such Resolution contains nothing affecting the rules and regulations of the Club. The Committee *shall* also call an Extraordinary General Meeting on the written requisition of twenty Members, not being of the Committee, under restrictions similar to the preceding.

, All notices of Extraordinary General Meetings, in virtue of this rule, issued by the Committee, must be signed by a majority of the Committee present specially summoned, and posted up in the public rooms of the Club for at least fourteen days previous to the day of meeting.

No new rule, or alteration of a general rule, shall

ever be made at an Extraordinary General Meeting, without the sanction of a majority of two-thirds of such Meeting, composed of at least fifty Members; nor unless the proposed new rule, or alteration of an old one, has been posted up in the usual place in the public rooms twenty-eight days previous to the day of meeting.

Meetings in General.

XXVIII.—No subject which does not relate to the management of the concerns of the Club shall ever be proposed, or brought forward for public discussion, at any Meetings of its Members; and notice of any proposition to be discussed shall be given and posted up in the Club-room fourteen days previous to the meeting. No subject which has been discussed at a General Meeting, and negatived by a majority equal to two-thirds of the number present, shall be brought forward again within a less period than one year. All questions affecting the character or conduct of Members when brought before a Meeting, to be decided by a ballot taken on the spot. All other questions to be decided by a show of hands as heretofore.

Miscellaneous.

XXIX.—The Club-house shall be open and ready for the reception of Members at eight o'clock on each morning from Lady-day to Michaelmas, and at nine o'clock from Michaelmas to Lady-day; and for Ingress shall be closed at two o'clock the next morning. No game shall be commenced nor refreshments supplied after half-past three o'clock, and every Member must leave the house by four o'clock, at which hour the Club is to be finally closed.*

XXX.—No Member shall give any money or gratuity to any of the servants of the Establishment upon any pretence whatever.

XXXI.—No Member shall take away from the Club, upon any pretence whatever, any newspaper, book, pamphlet, or other article, the property of the Institution.

XXXII.—A room shall be appropriated for the accommodation of dining a limited number of visitors, friends of the Members, subject to such rules and regulations as shall be hereafter adopted by the Committee for the time being.

No Visitor to be admitted to the Card room, on any pretence whatever.

No Visitor to be admitted to the Billiard and Smoking rooms from the Saturday preceding the Derby week until the Monday following the same,

* This Rule not to be applicable to the Derby Week.

both days inclusive, unless he has dined on the same day with a Member in the Club.

No Visitor is to be admitted to the Billiard rooms who has not on the same day dined with a Member in the Club.

XXXIII.—No provisions cooked in the Club-house, wines, or other liquors, shall be sent out of the house for the use of any Member.

XXXIV.—All complaints respecting breakfasts and dinners shall be stated on the back of the bill, and signed by the Member complaining, for the notice of the Committee; to whom also all complaints respecting the servants, or domestic arrangements of the Club shall be addressed.

XXXV.—All Members are required to pay their bills, for every expense they incur in the Club, *before they leave the house*, the Steward having positive orders not to open accounts with any individual, and being under the necessity of accounting to the Committee weekly for all monies passing through his hands.

XXXVI.—No game of hazard shall on any account be ever played in the Club-house, nor cards or other games allowed on Sundays.

No higher stake than one guinea points shall ever be played for.

Any deviation from the two last-mentioned rules shall render the Member liable to expulsion.

The Committee, upon a representation of the same being laid before them, are empowered to take cognizance of any debt of honor contracted in the Club, dealing with it solely according to Rule IV.

No Member shall on any account take a dog into the house.

No smoking shall be permitted in the house unless specially sanctioned by the Committee.

XXXVII.—A Library shall be formed, under *Library.* the direction of the Committee, to the extent of the funds set apart for that purpose and shall be open to the contributions of the Members, whose names shall be recorded.

XXXVIII.—Any infraction of the rules and regulations of the Club shall be taken immediate cognizance of by the Committee.

Each Member shall communicate his address, *or that of his banker or agent*, from time to time to the Secretary; and all notices sent to such address shall be considered as duly delivered.

These Rules and Regulations shall be printed,

and a copy of them, together with a list of the Committee and Members, shall be delivered to every Member, or transmitted to his address; but no Member shall be absolved from the effect of these rules on any allegation of not having received them.

Members compliance with the Rules.

XXXIX.—As the payment of the Subscriptions, according to the regulations, will entitle the Member to enjoy every benefit and privilege of the Club, such payment shall be his distinct acknowledgment of, and acquiescence in the rules and regulations of the Society.

Members newly elected.

XL.—On the admission of each new Member, the Secretary shall notify the same to him, in duplicate if abroad, with a copy of the regulations, and request him to instruct his agent or banker to pay his subscriptions.

THOMAS WALCOT, *Secretary.*

N.B.—All Letters addressed by Members to the Secretary of the Club must be post-paid.

ALPHABETICAL LIST.

A.

1859.	Abbott, Charles T., *M.B.*, Surgeon 39th Regt.
O.M.	Abbott, W. W., late Captain 36th Regiment
1856.	Acton, Charles, Captain 51st Light Infantry
1855.	Acton, Edw. W. F., Lieut. 76th Regiment
1853.	Acton, W. M. Cole., Captain H.P. 77th Regiment
1840.	Adam, William, late Captain 48th Regiment
1846.	Adams, Edw., Lt. Colonel Adj. R. Mil. Asylum
O.M.	Adams, Joseph H., Commissary-Gen. half-pay
1855.	Addington, Hon. C. J., Major 38th Regiment
1848.	Addington, Hon. W. W., late Lieut. Royal Navy
1851.	Adlington, H. S., late Capt. 4th Light Dragoons
1841.	Agnew, Sir A., Bart., M.P. late Capt 4th Lt.Drgs.
1860.	Agnis, John C., Assis.-Sur. Royal Horse Guards
1850.	Aidé, C. H., late Captain 85th Light Infantry
1839.	Ailsa, A., Marquis of, late Lieut. 17th Lancers
1848.	Aitken, Alex., late Captain 77th Regiment
1854.	Aldridge, John., Major 21st Fusiliers

1858.   Alexander, Boyd. F., Captain Rifle Brigade

1856.   Alexander, Claud, Lieut.-Col. Grenadier Guards

1857.   Alexander, Henry, Captain 1st Dragoon Guards

1860.   Alexander, John, H. I., Commander Rl. Navy

1855.   Alison, Fred. M., Major 19th Regiment

1842.   Allan, Andrew T., Lieut.-Colonel 25th Regiment

1857.   Allan, William, Captain 41st Regiment

1853.   Allen, Charles J. W., Captain 12th Lancers

1858.   Allfrey, Goodrich H., Capt. 2nd Dragoon Gds.

1841.   Allgood, L. J. H., late Lieut. 13th Lt. Drgs.

O.M.   Alves, John, Major-General, retired full pay

1846.   Ambrose, George James, Lt.-Colonel 3rd Buffs

1839.   Ambrose, John A., late Lieut. 76th Regiment

1850.   Amphlett, E., late Lieutenant 2nd Dragoons

1845.   Amsinck, William, Major, late 53rd Regiment

1842.   Anderson, George, Staff-Surgeon-Major

1853.   Anderson, J. H., late Captain 1st Dragoon Gds.

1851.   Anderson, Thomas, Major 64th Regiment

1851.   Anderson, W. H., Commander Royal Navy

1846.   Anderton W. I., late Lieutenant 17th Lancers

1859.   Annesley, Arthur L., Captain 11th Hussars

1850.   Annesley, Hon. A. A., late Lieut. 10th Hussars

1858.   Annesley, Stepn. F. C., Lt.-Col. 10th Regiment

1858.   Anson, Hon., A. H., *V.C.*, Major 7th Hussars

1844.   Antrobus, Philip, late Lieutenant 8th Regiment

1857.   Anstey, Edward, F., late Capt. 20th Regiment

1855.   Appleyard, Frederick E., Major Depôt Batt.

1858. Arbuckle, E. K. Vaughan, Captain 3rd Buffs
1854. Arbuthnot, Charles G., Major R. H. Artillery
1859. Arbuthnot, Hy. Thos., Captain Royal Artillery
1853. Arbuthnot, W. W., Captain 18th Hussars
1848. Archdall, A. M., Captain H.P. Royal Artillery
1846. Archdall, M., *M.P.*, late Capt. 50th Regiment
O.M. Archer, Clement R., late Capt. 4th Dragoon Gds.
O.M. Archer, William H., Major, late 16th Lancers
1845. Arkwright, Aug. P., Commander Royal Navy
1846. Arkwright, C., late Lieut. 1st Dragoon Guards
1838. Arkwright, F. W., late Capt. 4th Dragoon Gds.
1840. Arkwright, R. W., late Lieut. 7th Dragoon Gds.
1857. Armit, J. H., late Lieutenant 24th Regiment
1845. Armytage, William, Captain Royal Navy
O.M. Arney, Charles Augustus, Colonel unattached
O.M. Arthur, Sir Fred. L., Bart., Lieut.-Colonel unatt.
O.M. Ashmore, Charles, Major-General
1850. Ashworth, F. C., late Captain 19th Regiment
1858. Ashby, G. Ashby, late Captain 11th Hussars
1853. Atchison, G. T. H., Captain 67th Regiment
1843. Atchison, Henry Alexander, Capt. unattached
1856. Atherley, E. G. Eliot, Captain 45th Regiment
1850. Atkinson, Edward D., Lt.-Colonel 37th Regt.
1855. Atkinson Richard, Captain 12th Regiment
1858. Atkinson, William, Captain 13th Lt. Dragoons
1854. Attye, Francis L. O., Captain 2nd Regiment
O.M. Aubin, P., Lieut-Colonel 57th Reg. ret. full pay

1850.   Austen, Charles W., Lt.-Colonel 83rd Regiment
O.M.   Austin, William, Major, late 56th Regiment
1851.   Aytoun, James, Captain 7th Hussars

B.

1838.	Bacon, Henry H., late Capt. 3rd Dragoon Gds.
1850.	Baddeley, J. F. L., Major Royal Artillery
1849.	Bailie, James, Major 87th Fusiliers
1858.	Bailie, William Alex., Captain 82nd Regiment
1859.	Baillie, J. Baillie, late Lieut. Coldstream Gds.
O.M.	Bain, G., Dep. Assis. Commissary General H.P.
1851.	Bain, W., *M.D.*, Surgeon H.P. 34th Regiment
1855.	Baird, Sir David, Bart., Major late 98th Regt.
1859.	Baird, John K. E., Commander Royal Navy
1847.	Baird, Robert H., late Lieutenant Rifle Brigade
1848.	Baker, Henry, Commander Royal Navy
1842.	Baker, Henry J. B. T., late Lieut. 4th Drg. Gds.
1854.	Baker, Valentine, Lieut.-Colonel 10th Hussars
1855.	Balfour, Charles I., Commander Royal Navy
1855.	Balfour, Francis W., Major, late Rifle Brigade
1858.	Balfour, Henry Lowther, Capt. Royal Artillery
1851.	Balfour, J. W., late Captain 7th Dragoon Gds.
1840.	Balfour, T. G., *M.D.*, Deputy-Inspector-Gen.
1851.	Balguy, Henry, late Captain 4th Regiment
1848.	Ballard, James B., Commander Royal Navy
1859.	Bally, William, Lieutenant 33rd Regiment
1847.	Banon, Richard G. D., Surg.-Major 87th Fus.

1852.   Barber, H. H., late Lieutenant 17th Lancers
1852.   Barber, Lionel, C., Captain Royal Engineers
1846.   Barbor, Robert D., Major, late 40th Regiment
1851.   Barclay, David, Captain 16th Lancers
1859.   Baring, Henry, late Captain 17th Lancers
1855.   Barker, Francis O., *M.D.*, Staff Surgeon
1856.   Barlow, H. W., late Captain Royal Engineers
1849.   Barnes, Edward, late Captain 27th Regiment
1860.   Barnes, Richard Moore, Capt. 50th Regiment
O.M.   Barnes, W. E. Fitz-Edw., late Capt. 3rd Lt. Drgs.
1855.   Barnston, William, Major late 55th Regiment
1840.   Barron, F. B., Lieut.-Col. 3rd Dragoon Guards
1851.   Barron, Luke, *M.D.*, Staff Surgeon
1850.   Barron, William, late Captain 96th Regiment
1843.   Barrow, Thomas J. R., Lieutenant Royal Navy
O.M.   Barrow, Wallace, late Captain 17th Lancers
1841.   Barry, Rd. H. Smith, late Captain 12th Lancers
1858.   Barry, William H., Captain 73rd Regiment
1839.   Barry, W. N., late Lieutenant 8th Hussars
1855.   Barry, Wm. W., Lieut.-Col. Royal Artillery
1849.   Barstow, George, Major Royal Artillery
1858.   Barstow, Lewis, Lieutenant, Royal Navy
1856.   Bartholomew, G. C., Captain 10th Regiment
1843.   Bartley, John Cowell, Major 5th Fusiliers
1838.   Barton, Charles, Major, late 14th Lt. Dragoons
1848.   Barton, H. L., late Lieutenant 6th Dragoons
1859.   Barwell, Fredk. L., late Lieut. 50th Regiment

1853. Bassano, Alfred, Lieut.-Col. 32nd Light Infantry
1850. Bassett, William W., Captain 56th Regiment
1852. Bastard, B. J., late Lieutenant 9th Regiment
1841. Bastard, W. B., late Capt. 90th Light Infantry
1850. Batchellor, S. G., Capt. H.P. Royal Artillery
O.M. Bates, Henry, Colonel 98th Regiment
1854. Bates, Robert, Major 19th Regiment
1857. Bathurst, Henry, late Captain 23rd Fusiliers
1842. Bathurst, T. H., late Captain 75th Regiment
1858. Battiscombe, H. L., Captain 58th Regiment
1850. Baumgartner, T. M., Captain 83rd Regiment
O.M. Baxter, William, late Captain 30th Regiment
1851. Baynes, George E., Major 8th Regiment
1855. Baynes, H. J. le Marchant, Captain 88th Regt.
1850. Baynes, Robert S., Lieut.-Colonel unattached
1858. Beasley, Joseph N., Lieutenant 87th Regiment
1838. Beauclerk, Lord G. A., Major, late 6th Drg. Gds.
1858. Beaumont, G. W. Capt. Scots. Fusilier Guards
1850. Beaumont, Richard, Captain Royal Navy
1853. Becher, Sir Henry, Bt., late Lieut. Rifle Brigade
1853. Beckett, Hamilton, late Cornet 10th Hussars
1846. Bedford, R. T., Captain Royal Navy
1845. Bellairs, E. H. W., late Lieutenant 7th Fusiliers
1847. Bellairs, William, Major unattached
1851. Bellingham, W., late Captain 50th Regiment
1859. Bell, William M., Captain 3rd Light Dragoons
1838. Belson, Frederick, late Captain Rifle Brigade

1843.	Bence, E. R. S., late Capt. 1st Dragoon Guards
1857.	Bennett, W. C. F. B., Captain 6th Regiment
1850.	Bennett, F. W., late Captain 69th Regiment
1858.	Bennett, George, Lieut.-Colonel 20th Regiment
1850.	Bennett, Rev.T.W.,*B.A.*, Chaplain Royal Navy
1855.	Benson, Arthur E., late Lieut. 10th Hussars
1845.	Benson, Henry R., Colonel 17th Lancers
1846.	Bentinck, A. C., Lt.-Col. 4th Dragoon Guards
1838.	Beresford, Denis W. Pack, late Capt. Rl. Art.
1846.	Beresford, G. De la Poer, late Capt. 16th Regt.
1858.	Beresford, M. De la Poer, Captain 72nd Regt.
1858.	Berkeley, Henry W., Capt. 3rd Drg. Guards
1858.	Best, George H., Lieutenant 92nd Regiment
1847.	Bethune, Duncan M., Lt.-Col. 9th Regiment
1847.	Betson, W., Captain and Paym. 18th Hussars
1854.	Betts, George, Captain 81st Regiment
1857.	Betty, Joshua F., Captain Royal Artillery
1856.	Betty, W. T., Captain 6th Dragoon Guards
1859.	Bevan, Charles D., Lieutenant Royal Artillery
1855.	Bickerstaff, R., Lt.-Col. late 6th Dragoon Gds.
1849.	Biddle, Waring B., Captain 36th Regiment
1858.	Biddulph, Robert, Captain Royal Artillery
1844.	Bidgood, Thomas E., late Lieut. 1st Royals
1840.	Bill, Charles, late Lieutenant 6th Dragoons
1848.	Bird, H. C., late Capt. Ceylon Rifle Regiment
1851.	Bird, W. O., Captain 6th Dragoon Guards
O.M.	Biscoe, G. G., Lt.-Col. 66th Regt. ret. full-pay

1845. Bisset, M. Fenwick, late Lieut. 1st Drg. Gds.
1847. Bisshopp, Sir G. C., Bart., late Capt 12th Regt.
O.M. Black, George, Lieut.-Colonel late 75th Regt.
1838. Blackall, N. E., late Lieut. 90th Light Infantry
1851. Blackett, C. E., Captain Coldstream Guards
1853. Blackett, E. A., Lieutenant Royal Navy
1853. Blackett, E. W., Captain Rifle Brigade
1860. Blackett, William, Captain 61st Regiment
1852. Blair, E. S., late Lieut. 13th Light Dragoons
1856. Blair, W. S., Colonel H.P. Royal Artillery
1847. Blake, Patrick J., Captain Royal Navy
1855. Blake, Step., Major & Paym. 93rd Highlanders.
1854. Blakely, T. A., Captain H.P. Royal Artillery
1850. Bland, Alleyne, Commander Royal Navy
1853. Bland, James F., Captain 76th Regiment
1842. Blandy, Adam, late Lieut. 6th Dragoon Guards
1838. Blane, George, Commander Royal Navy
1843. Blaythwayt, G. W., late Capt. 1st Drg. Gds.
1850. Blewitt, Charles, Captain 65th Regiment
1852. Bligh, Frederick C., Major 41st Regiment
1847. Blosse, W. C. L., Captain Royal Artillery
1851. Blyth, W. D'U., Captain 14th Light Dragoons
1853. Boggis, J. E., Captain H.P. 55th Regiment
1849. Boldero, George N., Major 21st Fusiliers
1847. Bolton, A. S., late Captain 57th Regiment
1850. Bolton, John L., Captain Royal Artillery
1856. Bolton, R. G. B., late Lieut. Royal Horse Guards

1856. Bolton, Theophilus, Captain 22nd Regiment

1848. Bond, E., Lieut.-Col. late Prov. Depôt Battalion

1852. Bond, J. W., *M.P.*, late Lieut. 49th Regiment

1854. Bond, Ralph S., late Captain 14th Regiment

1859. Bonham, Francis, Captain 71st Regiment

1847. Bonham, C. W., Commander Royal Navy

1848. Bontine, W. C., late Cornet 2nd Dragoons

1859. Booth, Henry J. P., Major 43rd Regiment

O.M. Booth, William, Major-General

1854. Booth, William, Captain Royal Artillery

1850. Borrow, John, Major 18th Regiment

1851. Borthwick, R., late Lieutenant 91st Regiment

O.M. Borton, Arthur, *C.B.*, Colonel Depôt Battalion

1848. Bostock, J. A., *M.D.* Surg.-Major Scots Fus. Gds.

1855. Bott, Thomas, Major 6th Dragoon Guards

1838. Boucherett, Henry R., late Capt. 17th Lancers

1856. Boultbee, Henry T., late Captain Royal Artillery

1858. Bourbel, de A. A., Lieut. 6th Dragoon Guards

1842. Bourchier, C. J., late Capt. Coldstream Guards

1854. Bourchier, Claud T., *V.C.*, Major Rifle Brigade

1847. Bourchier, J. J., Major 52nd Light Infantry

1847. Bourke, Hon. John J., Lieut.-Col. unattached

1842. Bouverie, F. W. P., Commander Royal Navy

O.M. Bowdoin, J. T., late Capt. 4th Dragoon Guards

1858. Bowlby, Alfred P., Major 64th Regiment

1848. Bowles, Edward, Captain 60th Rifles

1838. Bowles, Henry O., late Captain 15th Regiment

1851.   Boyd, Edward, Captain 5th Lancers
1858.   Boyd, J. G. Hay, Major unattached
O.M.   Boyd, Walter, late Captain 87th Fusiliers
1850.   Boyes, C. R., *M.D.* Staff-Surgeon 1st Class
1851.   Boyle, Hon. E. J., Captain 85th Light Infantry
1851.   Boyle, Robert, Captain Royal Artillery
1842.   Boyle, William, Lieut.-Colonel 89th Regiment
1851.   Boyle, Hon. W. G., Major Coldstream Guards
1847.   Brabazon, Hugh B., Major, late Military Train
1848.   Bradford, Edward, Staff-Surgeon 1st class
1858.   Bradbury, Emanuel, Captain 1st Drg. Guards
1840.   Bragge, William, Colonel, late 37th Regiment
1853.   Bramly, Richard J., late Captain Cape M. Rifles
1851.   Bramston, T. H., Captain Grenadier Guards
1853.   Brandreth, C., late Lieut. 4th Light Dragoons
1846.   Brandreth, Thomas, Commander Royal Navy
1858.   Branfill, Benj. A., Captain 86th Regiment
1859.   Bravo, Alexandre, Captain 1st W. India Regt.
1853.   Bray, Edward W., Captain 83rd Regiment
1848.   Brenchley, H., late Captain 31st Regiment
1855.   Brendon, Algernon, Major Royal Artillery
1849.   Brereton, Godfrey, Commander Royal Navy
1853.   Breslin, W. J., *M.D.*, Staff-Surgeon, half-pay
1852.   Breton, John, Captain unattached
1853.   Breton, Peter W., late Captain 38th Regiment
1841.   Brett, Henry, Captain 18th Hussars
1839.   Brett, John, late Captain 15th Hussars

O.M.   Brett, John D., Major, late 17th Lancers

1847.   Brett, William F., Lieut.-Col. 54th Regiment

1847.   Brewster, William B., late Capt. Rifle Brigade

1853.   Bridge, G. J., late Captain 1st Dragoon Guards

1844.   Briggs, George, Major, late 1st Dragoon Gds.

1851.   Bright, Robert O., Lieut.-Col. 19th Regiment

1853.   Brigstocke, G. C., late Capt. 4th Dragoon Gds.

1852.   Brinckman, T. H., late Captain 17th Regiment

1850.   Brine, Frederick, Captain Royal Engineers

1851.   Brine, George A., Lieutenant Royal Navy

1858.   Brine, Lindesay, Lieutenant Royal Navy

1838.   Bringhurst, J. H., Major, late 90th Lt. Infantry

1855.   Brisco, Musgrave D., late Captain 7th Hussars

1840.   Bristow, S., late Captain 54th Regiment

1848.   Brocas, Bernard, late Lieut. 6th Dragoon Gds.

1849.   Bromley, Charles, Commander Royal Navy

1841.   Brooke, A. Beresford, late Lieut. 23rd Fusiliers

1854.   Brooke. J. Brooke, late Capt. 88th Regiment

1859.   Brooke, J. H. Langford, late Capt. 95th Regt.

1853.   Brooke, Thomas, Colonel 12th Regiment

1855.   Brooksbank, A., late Captain 38th Regiment

1839.   Brotherton, W., late Lieutenant 11th Hussars

1842.   Broughton, P., late Capt. 3rd Dragoon Guards

1844.   Brown, Amyatt E., Captain 5th Lancers

1849.   Brown, E. J. V., Lieut-Colonel late 60th Rifles

1840.   Brown, George J., Lt.-Col. 4th Light Dragoons

1846.   Brown, N. R., Colonel 34th Regt. ret. full-pay

1844.	Brown, Robert J., Capt. 14th Light Dragoons
1839.	Brown, William G., Colonel 24th Regiment
1843.	Browne, Alexander, *M.D.*, Surgeon half-pay
1859.	Browne, A. S. M., Captain 2nd Dragoons
1853.	Browne, C. A. G., Capt. 4th Light Dragoons
1859.	Browne, C. Edwd. Gore, Lieut. 25th Regt.
1850.	Browne, Charles F., Captain 35th Regiment
1838.	Browne, George, Major, late 35th Regiment
1854.	Browne, George R., Major 88th Regiment
1841.	Browne, W. R., late Captain 7th Fusiliers
1860.	Browning, Montagu C., Captain 89th Regt.
1856.	Bruce, Alexander C., Captain 91st Regiment
1846.	Bruce, Robert, Lieut.-Colonel 2nd Regiment
1849.	Bruce, Robert, Lieutenant-Colonel unattached
1852.	Bruce, William J., Captain 94th Regiment
1852.	Brumell, William, Major & Paymaster 25th Regt.
1846.	Brush, J. R., *M.D.*, Staff Surgeon 2nd Class
1846.	Bryson, Alexander, *M.D.* F.R.S., Inspector of Hospitals and Fleets
1855.	Buchan, G. W., Fordyce-, Col. late R. H. Gds.
1847.	Buchanan, D. C. R. C., late Cornet 2nd Drgs.
1853.	Buchanan, George, Captain 2nd Dragoons
1850.	Buchanan, N. G., late Capt. 93rd Highlanders
1852.	Buchanan, R. D., late Captain 72nd Highlanders
1859.	Buckle, Charles M., Commander Royal Navy
1858.	Buckley, Cecil W., *V.C.*, Commander Royal Navy
1846.	Bull, John James, LieutColonel 56th Regiment

1845. Bullen, Charles, Lieutenant Royal Navy
1856. Buller, Edmund M., Major Rifle Brigade
1852. Bulwer, E. G., *C.B.*, Lieut.-Col. 23rd Fusiliers
1860. Bunbury, Charles Thos , Lieut. Rifle Brigade
1839. Bunbury, Charles T. V., Major 82nd Regt.
1838. Bunbury, H. W., *C.B.*, Col. H.P. 23rd Fusiliers
1844. Bunbury, Philip, late Capt. 7th Dragoon Gds.
1846. Burke, John Hardman, Major 3rd Buffs
1859. Burnand, A., late Captain 17th Lancers
1853. Burnand, G. S., Captain 5th Dragoon Guards
1846. Burne, Godfrey J., Captain 73rd Regiment
1858. Burningham, H. G. C., Captain 58th Regt.
1858. Burnside, F. R. E., Captain 21st Fusiliers
1853. Burroughs, F. W., Major 93rd Highlanders
1855. Burrowes, Thomas A., Captain 45th Regiment
1848. Burton, A. W. D., *C.B.* Major 7th Drg. Gds.
1844. Burton, Sir C. W. C., Bt., late Lt. 1st Dragoons
1855. Bury, Hon. Alfred, late Captain 10th Regiment
1853. Busby, John, late Captain 13th Light Infantry
1856. Bushe, William D., Lieut.-Colonel 7th Hussars
1850. Butler, A. S., late Captain 36th Regiment
1846. Butler, Edward C., Major 36th Regiment
1853. Butler, Henry W., late Captain 15th Regiment
1846. Butler, Percy A., Lt.-Colonel 28th Regiment
1841. Butler, Thomas, late Lieutenant 7th Fusiliers
1849. Butler, Webbe, Lieutenant-Colonel 60th Rifles
1858. Butts, Fredk. John, Captain 77th Regiment

1848.   Butt, Thomas B., Lieut.-Col. 79th Highlanders
1846.   Byam, Edward G., late Captain 59th Regiment
1838.   Byrne, Thomas, Lieut.-Colonel 10th Regiment
1852.   Byrne, Thomas E., Captain Royal Artillery
1857.   Byron, John, Captain 10th Regiment
1852.   Bythesea, John, *V.C.*, Commander Royal Navy

C.

1850. Cambridge, H.R.H. Duke of, *K.G.*, *G.C.B.*, *K.P.*, *G.C.M.G.*, General Commanding-in-Chief ; Colonel Scots Fusilier Guards, &c., &c., PRESIDENT

1855. Caddy, John T., *M.D.*, Surgeon Royal Navy

1852. Cahill, A. P., *M.D.*, Surgeon 6th Regiment

1857. Calcott, C. R. B., Captain 26th Regiment

1841. Caldwell, Henry, *C.B.*, Captain Royal Navy

1845. Callaghan, F. M., late Lieutenant 60th Rifles

1851. Calthorpe, Hon. S. J. G., Major 5th Drag. Gds.

1847. Calvert, A. M., Captain Royal Horse Artillery

1854. Calvert, Charles, late Lieut. 43rd Light Infantry

1845. Calvert, C. W., late Capt. 2nd Dragoon Guards

1856. Cameron, A. S., Captain 25th Regiment

1846. Cameron, W. G., Major 4th Regiment

1854. Campbell, Sir A., Bart., Lieutenant Royal Navy

1858. Campbell, A. C., Lt.-Col. Scots Fusilier Grds.

1838. Campbell, Archibald J., late Capt. 44th Regt.

1849. Campbell, A. M., late Capt. 6th Dragoon Gds.

1841. Campbell, Charles F., Major, late 87th Fusiliers

1853. Campbell, Colin A., Commander Royal Navy

1855. Campbell, Colin F., Lieut.-Colonel 46th Regt.

1852. Campbell, Donald P.; late Capt. 92nd Highlanders
1849. Campbell, Duncan, Major, unattached
1852. Campbell, Fred., Major Cape Mounted Rifles
1847. Campbell, Frederick A., Captain Royal Navy
1856. Campbell, G., late Captain 71st Highlanders
1851. Campbell, H. J. M., Capt. H.P. Royal Artillery
1853. Campbell, James C., Commander Royal Navy
1854. Campbell, John A. G., late Captain 1st Royals
1858. Campbell, Jno. Henry, Lieutenant 33rd Regt.
1838. Campbell, John L., late Lieut. 5th Fusiliers
1849. Campbell, Patrick J., Captain Royal Artillery
1841. Campbell, Robert, late 32nd Regiment
1852. Campbell, Robert, Lieutenant Royal Navy
1852. Campbell, Robert, Captain 12th Lancers
1855. Campbell, Thomas M., Lieutenant Royal Navy
1851. Cane M., late Captain 89th Regiment
1839. Canning, C. P. Gordon, late Lieut. 78th Regt.
1848. Capel, C., late Lieutenant 75th Regiment
1838. Carden, Charles W., late Capt. 36th Regiment
1851. Cardew, C. B., late Captain 6th Dragoon Gds.
1848. Carew, C. H., late Lieutenant 2nd Life Guards
1851. Carew, G. H. W., late Capt. 1st Dragoon Gds.
1850. Carew, Robert H., late Captain 36th Regiment
O.M. Carey, Le Marchant, late Capt. 76th Regiment
1852. Cary, Hon. L. W. C., late Capt. 96th Regiment
1839. Carleton, William, Captain Royal Navy
1850. Carlyon, G. G., late Captain 1st Royals

D

1845.   Carlyon, T. T. S., Major, late 3rd Drag. Gds.
1850.   Carmichael, G. L., Major 95th Regiment
O.M.   Carmichael, Sir J. R., Bart., late Lt. 1st W.I.R.
1853.   Carnegie, Hon. Charles, late Lieut. 27th Regt.
1855.   Carnegie, Hon. John, Lieutenant Royal Navy
1859.   Carnegy, P. A. W., late Captain 15th Hussars
1851.   Carpenter, Charles, Captain Royal Artillery
1854.   Carpenter, G. W. Wallace, Major 7th Fusiliers
1845.   Cartan, William, Lieut.-Colonel, retired full pay
1848.   Carthew, Edmund J., Major Royal Artillery
1857.   Cass, Arthur H., Captain 10th Hussars
1838.   Cathcart, Andrew, late Captain 11th Hussars
1855.   Cathcart, Hon. A,. Lt.-Colonel 96th Regiment
1855.   Cathcart, Robert, late Lieut. 74th Highlanders
1856.   Cator, Ralph P., Commander Royal Navy
1839.   Cavan, Philip C., Lt.-Colonel late 30th Regt.
1846.   Cave, L. T., late Captain 54th Regiment
1838.   Cavendish, Hon. F., late Capt. 20th Regiment
1848.   Cazalet, G. II., late Captain 33rd Regiment
1856.   Chadwick, John De H., Lieut. late 9th Lancers
1860.   Chadwick Robert, Lieut. 14th Light Dragoons
1845.   Chaloner, Thomas, Captain Royal Navy
1849.   Chambers, E. J., late Lieut. 17th Regiment
1845.   Chambré, William, Colonel unattached
1858.   Chamberlayne, D. T., late Capt. 13th Lt. Drg.
1847.   Chaplin, Frank, Major 3rd Dragoon Guards

1841. Chapman, F. E., *C.B.*, Colonel, Deputy-Adjutant General Royal Engineers

1855. Chapman, G. H. J. M., Captain 5th Fusiliers

1854. Charlton, St. John W. C., late Capt. 1st Drgs.

1856. Charlton, Richard G., Captain 81st Regiment

1845. Charter, Ellis James, Major Depôt Battalion

1855. Chatfield, Alfred J., Lieutenant Royal Navy

O.M. Chearnley, W., late Captain 8th Regiment

1847. Chetwode, George, Lieut.-Col. late 8th Hussars

1841. Chetwode, R., Colonel H.P. 3rd Drag. Guards

1843. Chichester, Lord John, late Captain 87th Regt.

1848. Chichester, Nugent, late Captain 99th Regt.

1855. Chichester, N. C., Captain 7th Drag. Guards

1854. Chichester, Robt. B., Captain 81st Regiment

1838. Chichester, Lord S. A., late Lieut. 90th Regt.

1852. Childs Joseph C., Major Royal Artillery

1853. Christie, George F., late Captain 15th Regiment

1858. Christian, Henry, Commander Royal Navy

1849. Chrystie, John A., late Captain 1st Royals

1850. Churchill, C. H. Spencer, Major 60th Rifles

1852. Chute, Trevor, Colonel 70th Regiment

1849. Clanmorris, John Lord, late Lieut. Rifle Brig.

1857. Clark, James A., Lieutenant 15th Hussars

1853. Clark, Thomas, Captain 24th Regiment

1846. Clarke, Andrew, Captain Royal Engineers

O.M. Clarke, George C., Colonel 2nd Dragoons

1846. Clarke, J. W., late Captain 10th Hussars

1857. Clarke, M. de S. Mc. G., Lieut. 50th Regt.

1854. Clarke, Somerset M., Captain 29th Regiment

1844. Clarke, William, Colonel unattached

1851. Clay, George, Captain 19th Regiment

1852, Clayton, J. W., late Capt. 13th Lt. Dragoons

1859. Cleeve, Stewart Alex., Capt. 51st Lt. Infantry

1849. Cleaveland, F. D., Colonel Royal Artillery

1855. Clerk, Godfrey, Major Rifle Brigade

1847. Clerk, Henry, Lieut.-Colonel Royal Artillery

1838. Clerk, Mildmay, late Captain 12th Lancers

1852. Cleveland, G. D. D., Major 98th Regiment

1847. Clifford, Miller, Major Royal Artillery

1855. Clifton, Aug. W., late Captain Rifle Brigade

1849. Clifton, Chandos, F., Major 12th Lancers.

1847. Clifton, Thomas H., Lieut.-Col. unattached

O.M. Cloeté, Sir A. J., *C.B.*, *K.H.*, Major-General

1859. Close, Francis A., Commander Royal Navy

1859. Close, V. H., late Captain 90th Regiment

1858. Clowes, George, Major 8th Hussars

1848. Clutterbuck, D. H., late Captain 8th Hussars

1856. Clutterbuck, J. E. *M.D.* Surgeon 17th Regt.

1848. Coape, C., late Captain 67th Regiment

1854. Coates, Frederick, Captain 10th Hussars

1845. Cobbe, Alexander H., Major 87th Fusiliers

1843. Cobbe, C. A., late Captain 3rd Buffs

1848. Cochrane, James D., late Capt. 19th Regiment

O.M. Cockburn, Alexander, Captain unattached

1845. Cockburn, James H., Captain Royal Navy
1855. Cockburn, T. Hugh, Major 43rd Light Infantry
1848. Cocks, O. Yorke, Major 4th Regiment
1841. Cocks, P. R., Colonel H.P. Royal Artillery
1839. Cocksedge, Henry L., late Lieut. 6th Drg. Grds.
1842. Colborne, Hon. F., *C.B.*, Col. 6th Regiment
1840. Colborne, Hon. James, Lieut.-Col. unattached
1842. Cole, John A., Lieut.-Colonel 15th Regiment
1852. Coleman, Henry F. G., Captain 1st Dragoons
O.M. Coles, Josias R. J., Lieut.-Col. late 9th Lancers
1842. Collette, Henry, Major 67th Regiment
1846. Collier, George B. B., Lieutenant Royal Navy
1859. Collins, Edward A., Captain 26th Regiment
1847. Colmore, C. F. C., late Lieutenant 7th Hussars
1859. Colquhoun, H. M. L., Captain 77th Regiment
1841. Colquitt, J. Wallace, Captain H.P. 34th Regt.
1844. Colston, Edward, late Lieutenant 15th Hussars
1846. Colt, Charles Russell, Captain 56th Regiment
1850. Colthurst, David L., Major 17th Regiment
1851. Colthurst, Robert E., late Captain 48th Regt.
O.M. Colvile, Henry, Lieutenant-General
1844. Colville, Hon. W. J., Major Rifle Brigade
1855. Commerell, John E., *V.C.*, Captain Royal Navy
1843. Compton, Lord William, Captain Royal Navy
1853. Coney, Arthur H., Captain 67th Regiment
1852. Coney, Walter John, Captain 1st Dragoons

1839.   Congreve, George, *C.B.*, Major-General
1858.   Congreve, William, Captain 4th Regiment
O.M.   Connel, A. James N., *M.D.*, Surgeon half-pay
O.M.   Conolly, James, Lieutenant-Colonel unattached
1842.   Conolly, T. R., late Lieutenant 25th Regiment
1858.   Conran, Marcell, Captain 56th Regiment
1851.   Conran, W. A., late Captain 56th Regiment
1841.   Conyers, Chas. Edward, Major H.P. 97th Regt.
1855.   Conyngham, Lord Francis N., *M.P.*, Lt. R. Navy
O.M.   Coode, Henry, Lieutenant Royal Navy
1848.   Cook, Edwin A., Major late 11th Hussars
1850.   Cooke, Edward B., Captain 83rd Regiment
O.M.   Cooke, John H., Lieut.-Col., late 21st Fusiliers
1841.   Cookes, George, Captain unattached
1859.   Cookesley, A. Foulkes, Dep.-Assist.-Com.-Gen.
1856.   Cookworthy, W. Spicer, Captain 60th Rifles
1855.   Cooper, Arthur, Captain 6th Dragoon Guards
O.M.   Cooper, David S., late Captain 1st Royals
1838.   Cooper, Henry, Colonel 45th Regiment
1842.   Cooper, W. H., late Lieutenant 75th Regiment
1846.   Cooper, William, Captain 70th Regiment
1849.   Coote, C. D., late Lieut. 52nd Light Infantry
1851.   Coote, Eyre, late Lieutenant 11th Hussars
1853.   Copinger, H., Lt.-Col., ret. full-pay, 16th Regt.
1852.   Copland, Alex. L., late Captain 57th Regiment
1855.   Copley, G. E., late Lieutenant 88th Regiment
1842.   Corbet, Sir V. R., Bt., late Lieut. R. Horse Gds.

1856. Corbett, Frank, late Captain 33rd Regiment
1855. Corbett, John, Captain Royal Navy
1858. Corbett, William, Major H.P. 52nd Regiment
1844. Cormick, John, Lieut.-Colonel 20th Regiment
O.M. Cornock, Isaac, late Lieut. 14th Lt. Dragoons
1853. Cornwall, George, Major late 93rd Highlanders
1852. Cornwallis, Fiennes, Major 4th Light Dragoons
1858. Corrance, George E., late Lieut. 76th Regt.
1859. Corrigan, Jno. Joseph, Captain 3rd Drg. Gds.
1860. Costello, Arthur R., late Captain 7th Drg. Gds.
1840. Cotton, Corbet, Colonel unattached
1842. Cotton H. C., late Captain 21st Fusiliers
1841. Courtenay, George W. C., Rear-Admiral
1855. Courtenay, R. W., Captain Royal Navy
1856. Coventry, St. John, Lieutenant Royal Navy
1858. Cowell, James D., Major 6th Dragoons
O.M. Cowley, Norman, late Lieut. 5th Dragoon Gds.
1857. Cowper, Andrew J., Captain 15th Regiment
1855. Cox, W. Hamilton, Major Royal Artillery
1856. Coxon, James H., Lieutenant Royal Navy
1857. Craster, James T., Captain 38th Regiment
1858. Craven, W. G., late Lieutenant 1st Life Guards
1858. Craven, Walter A. K., Lieutenant Royal Navy
1839. Crawfurd, Robert, late Captain 66th Regiment
1853. Crawford, Francis H., Captain 98th Regiment
1859. Crawford, Thomas, *M.D.*, Surgeon 18th Regt.
1844. Crawford, W. T., *C.B.*, Colonel Royal Artillery

1851. Crawley, H., late Lieutenant 1st Life Guards
1850. Crawley, P. S., Major Coldstream Guards
1854. Crawley, Thomas R., Lieut.-Colonel 6th Drgs.
1842. Crawshay, A., late Captain 17th Lancers
1849. Creagh, Charles O., Major 86th Regiment
1851. Crealock, H. H., Lieut.-Col. 90th Lt. Infantry
1859. Crealock, J. North, Captain 95th Regiment
1855. Crerar, James, Surgeon 60th Rifles
1855. Cresswell, George, Captain unattached
1858. Crewe, Evelyn H., Capt. 1st Dragoon Guards
1853. Creyke, A. S., Captain Royal Engineers
1852. Crofts, Edmund, late Captain 23rd Fusiliers
1859. Croker, William, Captain 27th Regiment
1849. Crombie, Alexander, Captain 72nd Highlanders
1851. Crookshank, Alex. C., Assist.-Com.-General
O.M. Crosbie, William, late Captain Rifle Brigade
1854. Crosse, Charles K., Major 52nd Light Infantry
1848. Crosse, Joshua Grant, Major 88th Regiment
1855. Crosse, John Hill, Captain 16th Regiment
1850. Crowe, J. W., late Lieutenant 83rd Regiment
1859. Cubitt, William, late Lieutenant 60th Rifles
O.M. Culpeper, J. Bishop, late Captain 14th Lt. Drgs.
1846. Cumberland, Octavius, Captain Royal Navy
1841. Cumming, Arthur, Captain Royal Navy
1840. Cumming, Sir A.P.G., Bt., late Capt. 4th Lt.Drgs.
1841. Cumming, H. W., Lt.-Col. late Coldstream Gds.
1853. Cunliffe, E. B., late Captain 6th Dragoons

1858. Cuningham, John, Captain 1st Dragoon Guards
1847. Cunningham, J., late Capt. 4th Dragoon Gds.
1858. Cunningham, John P., *M.D.*, Staff-Surgeon
1853. Cure, Alfred C., Lieut.-Col. Grenadier Guards
1843. Cureton, Edward Burgoyne, Major 12th Lancers
1855. Currie, Richard H., late Captain 6th Dragoons
1847. Currie, Samuel, *M.D.*, Dep.-Insp.-General
1841. Curry, Douglas, Captain Royal Navy
1860. Curtis, Fra. Geo. Savage, Capt. 6th Drg. Gds.
1850. Curtis, Constable, late Captain 12th Lancers
1849. Curtis, Reginald, Major Royal Artillery
1848. Curzon, Hon. E. G., Capt. 52nd Lt. Infantry
1847. Curzon, Hon. F., Commander Royal Navy
1847. Curzon, Hon. Leicester, Lt.-Col. Rifle Brigade
1845. Custance, W. N., *C.B.*, Colonel 6th Drg. Gds.
1858. Cuthbert, E. C., Captain Royal Artillery
1854. Cuthbert, John R. late Captain 6th Dragoons

D.

1839.   Dalgety, James W., Lieut.-Col. late 74th Regt.

1846.   Dallas, George Fred., Major 46th Regiment

O.M.   Dallas, Robert W., late Captain 2nd Drg. Gds.

O.M.   Dalrymple, Sir H., Bt., Lt.-Col., late 71st Regt.

1841.   Dalton, Charles J., Colonel Royal Artillery

1859.   Dalyell, O. W., Commander Royal Navy

1840.   Dane, Richard, *M.D.*, Dep. Inspector General

1839.   Daniel, Samuel, Paymaster Depôt Battalion

1846.   Daniell, C. F. Torrens, Major unattached

1838.   Daniell, Henry, Colonel, late Coldstream Gds.

1850.   Daniell, J. H., late Captain 42nd Highlanders

1856.   D'Arcy, William, late Captain 67th Regiment

1854.   Dare, F. M. Hall, Lieut., late 23rd Fusiliers

1841.   Darell, Henry J., Major, late 60th Rifles

O.M.   d'Arley, William W., Colonel R. A., ret. full pay

1855.   Dashwood, B. G., Captain 20th Regiment

1847.   Dashwood, F. L., late Captain 16th Lancers

1847.   Dashwood, W. H. A., late Captain 36th Regt.

1855.   Daubeny, Edward, Captain 67th Regiment

1855.   Daubeny, James, *C.B.*, Lieut.-Col. 62nd Regt.

1858.   Daubeney, Alfred G., Captain 7th Fusiliers

1855.   Davenport, A. H., late Lieut. 1st Life Guards

1842.	Davenport, W. D., Major late 26th Regiment
1857.	Davidson H. G., late Lieut. 78th Highlanders
1841.	Davidson, James, late Captain 6th Dragoons
1839.	Davie, Charles C., late Captain 67th Regiment
1846.	Davies, John, Staff-Surgeon-Major
1854.	Davies, Thomas, late Lieutenant 11th Regiment
1858.	Davies, Thomas, Commander Royal Navy
1850.	Davis, Gronow, *V.C.*, Major Royal Artillery
1859.	Davy, Daniel B., Lieutenant Rifle Brigade
1860.	Dawson, Arthur Fredk., late Captain 6th Drgs.
1859.	Dawson, Edwd., F., late Captain 6th Dragoons
1846.	Day, George F., *V.C.*, Commander Royal Navy
O.M.	Deacon, Charles, late Captain 9th Lancers
O.M.	Deacon, Charles C., *C.B.*, Colonel 46th Regt.
1852.	Deacon, W. E. D., Major 61st Regiment
1855.	Deane, G. O., late Lieutenant 22nd Regiment
1856.	Deane, Robert, late Lieutenant Royal Navy
1858.	Dearden, John, late Capt. 13th Light Dragoons
O.M.	De Blaquiere, John, Lord, late Capt. 41st Regt.
1845.	De Blaquiere, Hon. Wm. B., Commander R. Navy
1840.	De Butts, J. W., late Captain 74th Highlanders
1839.	De Crespigny, H. O., late Lieut. 20th Regt.
O.M.	De Lacy, John, Colonel late 39th Regiment
1858.	De Morel, C. C., Lieut.-Col. Depôt Battalion
1840.	Deedes, George, Major, late 35th Regiment
1855.	Deedes, William, Captain 30th Regiment
1848.	Delmè, George, Captain Royal Navy

1840.   Denison, C. A., Colonel 52nd Light Infantry

1852.   Denne, Lambert H., Captain R. Horse Artillery

1848.   Dennistoun, R., late Lieutenant 34th Regiment

O.M.   Denny, William, Colonel, late 71st Highlanders

1850.   Dent, Edward F., Commander Royal Navy

1854.   Dering, Edward C., late Lieut. 44th Regiment

1852.   De Robeck, J. H., Baron, late Capt. 4th Regt.

1858.   De Robeck, R. C. P., Captain 4th Regiment

1844.   De Rodes, Wm. H., late Cornet 1st Drg. Gds.

1841.   DeTeissier, J.F., Lt.-Col. Invalid Depôt Chatm.

1854.   De Trafford, Augustus, late Lieut. 1st Drgs.

1858.   Dettmar, Montague, late Captain 3rd Light Drgs.

1852.   Dew, Roderick, Captain Royal Navy

1847.   Dewar, A., late Captain 20th Regiment

1846.   De Windt, J. C., late Lieutenant 15th Hussars

1854.   De Winton, W., late Captain 1st Life Guards

1852.   Dick, Augustus A., Captain 29th Regiment

1855.   Dick, Charles C., late Lieut. 43rd Lt. Infantry

1855.   Dick, H. St. J., late Capt. 2nd Dragoon Gds.

1838.   Dickenson, Chas. F. B. G., late Capt. 34th Regt.

1854.   Dickens, Compton A. S., Major 12th Regiment

1840.   Dickson, S. A., *M.P.*, late Capt. 13th Lt. Drgs.

1848.   Dickson, William T., Lieut.-Col. 16th Lancers

1843.   Dod, Whitehall, late Captain 6th Dragoons

1839.   Doherty, C. Edm., Colonel late 13th Lt. Drgs.

O.M.   Doherty, H. E., *C.B.*, Colonel H.P. 9th Regt.

1856.   Domenichetti, R., *M.D.*, Surg. 75th Regiment

O.M. Domville, M. D. Taylor, late Lieut. 68th Regt.
1853. Domville, W. T., *M.D* , Surgeon Royal Navy
1850. Donovan, C. H., late Capt. 4th Dragoon Guards
1851. Donovan, T., late Lieut. 1st Dragoon Guards
1860. Dormer, Hon., J. B. J., Captain 74th Highland.
1858. Dormer, Hon. J.-C., Major 13th Lt. Infantry
1842. Dorrien, R. A. Smith, late Capt. 16th Lancers
1849. Douglas, Sir G. H., Bart., late Capt. 34th Regt.
1844. Douglas, Henry S., late Capt. 42nd Highlanders
1838. Douglas, John, *C.B.*, Colonel H.P. Depôt Batt.
1845. Douglas, Robert, Captain 23rd Fusiliers
1840. Douglas, William, Major 14th Regiment
1839. Douglas, William C., late Captain 17th Lancers
1854. Dowbiggen, E. T., late Captain 7th Drg. Gds.
1855. Dowbiggen, M. Hamilton, Major 99th Regt.
1858. Dowdeswell, W. F., Captain 7th Dragoon Gds.
1854. Downman, G. C., late Captain 66th Regiment
1845. D'Oyly, John W., Major 11th Regiment
1855. Drake J. C. T., Captaid 2nd Regiment
1841. Drake, W. W., late Captain 29th Regiment
1854. Drewe, Francis Edward, Major Depôt Battalion
1858. Drew, Browning, Captain 75th Regiment
1844. Draper, W. Gray, late Captain 3rd Lt. Dragoons
1847. Drought, G. W., late Capt. 51st Light Infantry
1853. Drummond, A. M., late Captain Rifle Brigade
1851. Drummond, H. M., late Capt. 42nd Highlanders
1852. Drummond, J., late Lieutenant 10th Hussars

1842. Drysdale, W., *C.B.*, Lieut.-Colonel 9th Lancers

1841. Duberly, Henry, Major & Paymaster 8th Hussars

1854. Dudgeon, James J., Captain 22nd Regiment.

1849. Dudgeon, Robert C., Captain 61st Regiment

O.M. Duff, Hon., G. S,. late Cornet Royal H. Guards

1858. Duff, James, late Major 23rd Fusiliers

1847. Duff, R. G., late Captain 12th Regiment

1853. Duff, Robert W., Major & Paymaster Depôt Batt.

1851. Dunbar, Arch. H., Captain 66th Regiment

1846. Dunbar, Edward D., late Captain 21st Fusiliers

1859. Dundas, Adam A. D., Lieutenant Royal Navy

1847. Dundas, Thomas, Captain 12th Regiment

1851. Dunlop, J., *M.D.*, Staff-Surgeon

1855. Dunlop, J. A. R., Commander Royal Navy

1855. Dunn, Alex. Robert, *V.C.*, Major 100th Regt.

1846. Du Plat, Charles T., Major Royal Artillery

1851. Durant, G. C., late Captain 12th Lancers

1853. Durnford, George, Col. 70th Regt. ret. full pay

1854. Dyce, Thomas R., Surgeon-Major 15th Regt.

1852. Dyke, Charles, Lieutenant Royal Navy

1858. Dyne, M. James B., Capt. 2nd Dragoon Gds.

1854. Dymond, Robert, Captain 3rd Light Dragoons

1847. Dynon, Patrick, Captain 16th Lancers

O.M. Dyson, Edwards, Major late 3rd Dragoon Gds.

1843. Dyson, J., Major Royal Artillery, retired full pay

O.M. Dyson, John D., Colonel late 3rd Dragoon Grds.

E.

1854. Earle, W. Henry, Captain 17th Regiment
1840. Eason, P., Major 61st Regiment, retired full pay
1859. East, Cecil James, Lieutenant 82nd Regiment
1851. East, C. W. Clayton, late Lieut. 15th Regiment
1858. Eaton, Henry P., Captain 60th Rifles
1858. Eden, Morton R., Captain 56th Regiment
1847. Edgell, G. R., late Captain 7th Fusiliers
1854. Edlmann, Joseph E., Captain 1st Dragoon Gds.
1839. Edwardes, Hume, late Captain 55th Regiment
1838. Edwards, Cadwallader, late Lieut. 29th Regt.
1848. Edwards, Herbert, late Captain 2nd Dragoons
1855. Edwards, S. H. H., Captain 98th Regiment
1850. Edwards, W. G., late Captain 10th Hussars
1851. Egerton, Chas. R., Commander Royal Navy
1839. Egerton, Francis P., Commander Royal Navy
1855. Egerton, Philip LeB., Capt. Coldstream Guards
1853. Egmont, George James, Earl of, Vice-Admiral
1856. Elgee, John L., Major Royal Artillery
1858. Elkington, J. H. F., Lieut.-Colonel 6th Regt.
1859. Elles, William K., Captain 38th Regiment
1850. Ellice, Charles H., *C.B.*, Colonel 24th Regiment
1850. Elliot, Alexander J. H., Major unattached

1848. Elliot, Hon. C. G. J. B., *C.B.*, Capt. Royal Navy

1845. Elliot, Hon. Gilbert, Major Rifle Brigade

1858. Elliot, John McDowell, Captain 4th Regiment

1859. Ellis, Arthur E. A., Captain 33rd Regiment

1849. Ellis, Frederick, Captain 9th Lancers

1847. Ellis, Henry Disney, Major Depôt Battalion

1839. Ellis, Powrie, Lieut.-Col. H.P. Royal Artillery

O.M. Ellis, William S. A., late Lieut. 9th Lancers

1855. Ellison, Richard George, Capt. 47th Regiment

1838. Elphinstone, John E. Lord, late Capt. 17th Lan.

1851. Elphinstone, W. B., Commander Royal Navy

1848. Elrington, F. R., Lieut-Colonel Rifle Brigade

1852. Elrington, Richd. J., Major & Paym. 10th Huss.

1851. Elwes, J. H. E., late Lieutenant 65th Regiment

1840. Elwes, L. C., late Lieutenant 11th Hussars

1853. Elwes, V. D. H. C., late Cornet 12th Lancers

1854. Ernst, Henry, late Captain 88th Regiment

1855. Erskine, David H., late Capt. 92nd Highlanders

O.M. Erskine, George, Col., Deputy-Insp. Volunteers

1859. Erskine, Henry D., Capt. Scots Fusilier Gds.

1846. Erskine, W. H. Kennedy, late Capt. 17th Lancers

1847. Espinasse, James W., Captain 12th Regiment

1860. Evans, John, Lieutenant 9th Lancers

1854. Evans, U. W., *M.D.*, Surgeon 15th Regiment

1851. Evatt, Henry A., late Lieut. Ceylon Rifle Regt.

1839. Evelegh, Geo. C., Capt. H.P. Royal Artillery

1848. Evelyn, G. P., late Captain Rifle Brigade

O.M.   Everard, Walling, late Captain 60th Rifles
1858.   Everett, John F., Captain 25th Regiment
1852.   Every, Sir Henry F., Bt., late Lieut. 90th Regt.
1853.   Ewart, Charles B., Major Royal Engineers
1845.   Ewart, Charles J. F., Captain Royal Navy
1856.   Ewart, W. S., Captain Grenadier Guards
1860.   Ewen, Arthur J. A., Lieut. 38th Regiment
1855.   Ewen, Charles, late Captain 65th Regiment
1838.   Eyton, William A., late Captain 96th Regiment

E

F.

1852.	Fairbairn, W. H., *M.D.*, Staff-Surgeon
1855.	Fairfax, Sir W. G. H. T., Bt., Captain 15th Reg.
1852.	Falconer, Hon. C. J. Keith, Maj. late 4th Lt. Drgs.
1858.	Fanning, Matthew, Captain 64th Regiment
1850.	Fanshawe, T. Basil, Captain 33rd Regiment
1849.	Farmer, Reginald O., Captain Royal Artillery
1847.	Farrell, F. A., late Lieutenant 7th Hussars
1842.	Farrer, James S. H., Major 84th Regiment
1860.	Farquharson, F. E. H., *V.C.*, Lieut. 42nd Regt.
1847.	Fearon, F. G. W., late Captain 63rd Regiment
1856.	Feilden, Henry B., Captain 6th Regiment
1854.	Feilden, O. Barton, Captain 78th Highlanders
1848.	Feilden, Randle J., Major 60th Rifles
1855.	Fellowes, Charles, Captain Royal Navy
1852.	Fellowes, Edward, Major unattached
1839.	Fellowes, James, late Lieutenant Royal Navy
1856.	Fellowes, T. H. B., Lieutenant Royal Navy
1842.	Fellowes, William A., Captain Royal Navy
1853.	Fenton, E. Dyne, Captain 86th Regiment
1849.	Fenwick, Percival, Lieut.-Col. 69th Regiment
1847.	Fenwick, William, *C.B.*. Colonel 10th Regiment
1845.	Fetherstonhaugh, J. H., late Capt. 11th Regt.

1856.	Fetherstonhaugh, W., Maj.&Pay. 14th Lt. Drgs.
1849.	Ffennell, James R., Surgeon 16th Regiment
1847.	Field, George T., Major Royal Artillery
1856.	Fiennes, Hon. J. De V., Major 7th Hussars
1846.	Finch, Hon. D. G., Major 24th Regiment
1855.	Finnie, William, Surgeon 1st Class half-pay
1858.	Fisher, E. R., Captain 4th Dragoon Guards
1858.	Fisher, Louis W., Lieutenant 82nd Regiment
1855.	Fitz-Gerald, G. R., late Lieut. Royal Navy
1849.	Fitz-Gerald, J., late Captain 87th Fusiliers
1851.	Fitz-Gerald, Lord Otho. late Lieut. R. H. Guards
1856.	Fitz-Gerald, Thomas G., Staff-Surgeon
1846.	Fitzgerald, William H. D., Major unattached
1859.	Fitzmaurice, Hon. A. T., late Lt. 72nd High.
1854.	Fitzmaurice, Hon. F. O'B., Lieut. Royal Navy
1848.	Fitzmaurice, Hon. H. W., late Capt. 72nd Regt.
1856.	Fitzmaurice, Hon. J. T., Lieut. Royal Navy
1855.	Fitz-Roy, Cavendish C., Capt. 68th Lt. Infantry
1844.	Fitz-Wygram, F. W. J., Lt.-Col. 15th Hussars
1846.	Fleming, E. J. I., late Captain 2nd Regiment
1856.	Fletcher, Alexander, Captain 12th Lancers
1853.	Fletcher, Francis C., Captain 60th Rifles
1854.	Flood, Fred. R. S., Major 82nd Regiment
1849.	Flower, C. S., late Lieutenant Rifle Brigade
1854.	Flower, Hon. H., late Lieut. 52nd Lt. Infantry
O.M.	Fogo, Jas., Major-Gen., ret. full pay R. Artillery
1857.	Fogo, James M. S., Surgeon Royal H. Artillery

1853.   Forbes, Charles S., Commander Royal Navy

1859.   Forbes, George, Major late 3rd Lt. Dragoons

1849.   Forbes, Thomas George, Captain Royal Navy

O.M.   Forbes, Thomas J., General Royal Artillery

O.M.   Forbes, William, Major unattached

1853.   Ford, Egerton, late Lieut. 14th Lt. Dragoons

1848.   Ford, F. C., late Lieut. 4th Light Dragoons

1856.   Forde, Matthew B., Captain Royal Artillery

1859.   Forde, Thomas Douglas, Capt. 46th Regiment

O.M.   Forrest, John H., late Captain 11th Hussars

1858.   Forster, Fred. B., Capt. & Paym. 5th Fusiliers

1840.   Forster, F. R., Major 4th Dragoon Guards

1848.   Forster, John, Major unattached

1844.   Fort, James, late Lieut. 5th Dragoon Guards

1846.   Fort, John, late Lieut. 5th Dragoon Guards

1850.   Forteath, Alex., *M.D.*, Surgeon 1st Dragoons

1846.   Fortescue, J. C. W., Lt.-Col. Royal Artillery

1841.   Foster, Charles J., Lieut.-Colonel 16th Lancers

1846.   Foster, James, late Lieut. 1st Dragoon Guards

1853.   Fowke, John S. F., Captain 54th Regiment

1844.   Fowler, George, C., Commander Royal Navy

O.M.   Fowler, Robert D., Commander Royal Navy

1847.   Fox, J. W., late Captain 12th Lancers

1845.   Frampton, H. J., Major, late 50th Regiment

O.M.   France, Henry H., late Captain 6th Drag. Gds.

1846.   Francis, Henry, Major 64th Regiment

1839.   Francis, Thomas J., Captain 3rd Dragoon Gds.

1838. Francklyn, Gilbert W., Colonel 17th Regiment
1850. Franklin, Henry, Staff-Surgeon-Major
1850. Franklyn, Charles, *C.B.*, Major-General
1848. Fraser, Hon. D. M'D., Lt.-Col. Royal Artillery
1858. Fraser, G. C., Major 11th Hussars
1858. Fraser, George, Captain 42nd Highlanders
1858. Fraser, Thomas, *M.D.*, Surgeon 10th Hussars
1860. Fraser, James Keith, Captain 1st Life Guards
1840. Fraser, W. K., late Captain 4th Light Dragoons
1859. Frederick, Arthur T., late Lieut. 5th Drg. Gds.
1846. Freeling, Arthur H., Lt.-Col. Royal Engineers
1853. Freeling, Sandford, Captain Royal Artillery
1859. Fremantle, Fitzroy W., Capt. Coldstream Gds.
1855. Freme, J. Herbert, late Capt. 79th Highlanders
1842. Freer, D. G., Major, late 3rd Buffs
O.M. Freer, John H., Maj.-Gen. Royal Artillery
1852. Fuller, C. F., late Lieutenant, 76th Regiment
1854. Fuller, W. R., late Lieutenant 53rd Regiment
1849. Fyfe, Douglas M., late Cornet 4th Lt. Dragoons

G.

1850.   Gage, Hon. E. T., Lieut.-Col. Royal Artillery
1852.   Gale, Henry R. H., Captain 90th Regiment
1840.   Gall, R. H., *C. B.*, Lt.-Col. 14th Light Drags.
O.M.   Gallwey, Henry J. W. S. P., Com. Royal Navy
O.M.   Gallwey, Philip P., late Capt. 90th Lt. Infantry
1841.   Galton, Douglas, Captain Royal Engineers
1846.   Galton, Herman E., late Capt. 50th Regiment
1856.   Gammell, J. H. H., Captain 9th Regiment
1847.   Gammie, Patrick, Deputy-Inspector-General
1858.   Gandy, Fredk., Lt.-Col. late Scots Fus. Grds.
1839.   Garden, Robert J., late Captain 45th Regiment
1855.   Gardiner, Sir R., *K.C.B.*, *K.C.H.*, Gen. Rl. Art.
1853.   Gardiner, Thomas G., Major unattached
1853.   Gardyne, T. M. B., late Lieut. 40th Regiment
1853.   Garforth, Frank, Captain 7th Hussars
1847.   Garforth, W. F. W., late Lieut. 68th Lt. Infantry
1852.   Garnett, Alfred J., late Captain 16th Regiment
1856.   Garrard, Robert, Captain 5th Dragoon Guards
O.M.   Garratt, Francis late Capt. 3rd Dragoon Guards
1844.   Garrett, Algernon R., Major 16th Regiment
1846.   Garvagh, Lord, late Captain 7th Hussars
1839.   Garvock, John, Colonel unattached
O.M.   Gascoyne, T. B., Capt. H.P. Ceylon Rifle Regt.

1847. George, J. L., late Lieutenant 37th Regiment
1856. George, Thorne G., Major & Paym. 4th Lt. Dgs.
1854. Gervis, Aug. T., late Lieut. 52nd Lt. Infantry
1845. Gibbon, James R., *C.B.*, Lt.-Col. Rl. Artillery
1854. Gibbs, Charles, Captain 2nd Regiment
1858. Gifford, John W. J., Captain 21st Regiment
1841. Gildea, Francis, late Lieutenant 66th Regiment
1841. Gildea, S. Mason, Major unattached
1858. Giles, James, Lieutenant 14th Light Dragoons
1851. Gill, Walter H., late Lieut. Cape Mounted Rifles
1847. Glanville, Francis R., Captain Royal Artillery
1852. Glover, John H., Lieutenant Royal Navy
1858. Glover, Robert, C., Captain 43rd Regiment
1850. Glubb, John W., late Captain 44th Regiment
1854. Glyn, Henry C., Commander Royal Navy
1848. Glyn, Julius R., *C.B.*, Lieut.-Col. Rifle Brigade
1858. Glyn, Robert Carr, Captain 7th Fusiliers
1848. Goad, C. W., late Lieut. 5th Dragoon Guards
1855. Goad, G. M., late Capt. 13th Light Dragoons
1854. Godby, Joseph, Major Royal Artillery
1860. Goddard, Fredk. F., Lieutenant 80th Regiment
1853. Godden, F. M., late Lieutenant 56th Regiment
1853. Godman, R. T., Captain 5th Dragoon Guards
1850. Goff, Robert, late Captain 16th Lancers
1854. Goff, Trevor, Captain unattached
1850. Goff, T. W., late Captain 7th Dragoon Guards
O.M. Goldsmid, Albert, Major-General

1858.   Gooch, Percy F., Captain 92nd Regiment

1856.   Gooch, Thomas S., Lieutenant Royal Navy

1855.   Goode, Winter, Major 64th Regiment

1847.   Goode, W. H., Major late 62nd Regiment

1841.   Goodenough, A. C., Colonel Depôt Battalion

1841.   Goodenough, H. P., Lt.-Colonel Royal Artillery

1852.   Goodenough, W. H., Major Royal Artillery

1859.   Goodricke, H. H., Captain 90th Regiment

1840.   Gordon, A., *M.D.*, *C.B.*, Dep.-Insp.-General

1850.   Gordon, C. A. Boswell, Major 60th Rifles

1852.   Gordon, Charles H., *C.B.*, Lt.-Col. Depôt Batt.

1855.   Gordon, H. G., *M.D.*, Surgeon 69th Regiment

1854.   Gordon, Sir W., Bart., Major 17th Lancers

1846.   Gordon, W. E. A., Captain Royal Navy

1848.   Gordon, Webster T., Major 66th Regiment

1844.   Gore, Annesley P., Major late 53rd Regiment

1858.   Gore, Augustus F. W., late Lieut. 7th Hussars

1860.   Gore, A. W. Knox, Captain 60th Rifles

1858.   Gore, Henry Pratt, Major 6th Regiment

1855.   Gore, Thomas, Major 88th Regiment

1848.   Goring, Sir Chas., Bart., late Lieut. 12th Lancers

1858.   Gosling, Robert, late Capt. 13th Lt. Infantry

O.M.   Gowan, George M., late Captain 97th Regiment

1860.   Gower, H. B. B. Leveson, Lieut. 80th Regt.

1847.   Gower, J. E. L., late Captain 50th Regiment

1860.   Grace, Sheffield, Captain, 68th Regiment

1840.   Graham, Allan H., Lt.-Col. Royal Artillery

1856.   Graham, Reginald H., Captain Rifle Brigade
1858.   Graham, Lumley, Lt.-Colonel 19th Regiment
1858.   Graham, John H., Major 22nd Regiment
1852.   Grain, Henry, Captain Royal Engineers
1842.   Grant, Archibald, late Capt. 4th Lt. Dragoons
1855.   Grant, Francis R. C., Captain 5th Lancers
1849.   Grant, Francis W., late Captain 16th Lancers
1850.   Grant, Henry J., Commander Royal Navy
1838.   Grant, Hon. James, late Lieut. 42nd Highlanders
1839.   Grant, John, late Captain 49th Regiment
1852.   Grant, J. J., Maj. Rl. Newfoundland Companies
1855.   Grant, John M., Captain Royal Engineers
1851.   Grant, Patrick J. J., Captain 96th Regiment
1841.   Grant, W. C., late Lieut. 1st Dragoon Guards
1840.   Grant, W. L., late Captain 7th Fusiliers
1854.   Granville, Bevill, Major 23rd Fusiliers
1855.   Granville, Robert, C., Captain 26th Regiment
1857.   Grape, H., Lieut. H.P. Royal Marines Lt. Inf.
1850.   Gratrex, T. P., Captain 13th Light Dragoons
1848.   Grattan, A. O'D., Major Royal Engineers
1849.   Grattan, J., *C.B.*, Colonel H.P. 18th Regiment
1844.   Graves, C. T., late Captain 92nd Highlanders
O.M.   Graves, John S., Deputy-Insperal-General
1847.   Gray, W., late Lieutenant 80th Regiment
1847.   Green, Andrew P. S., Major Royal Artillery
1851.   Green, Charles M., Major 30th Regiment
1857.   Green, Thomas E., Captain Military Train

O.M.   Greene, John, *M.P.*, late Lieut. 7th Drag. Gds.

1850.   Greene, Thomas, Captain Royal Navy

1844.   Greenwood, Joseph, Captain unattached

1860.   Greenwood, John Jas , Captain 33rd Regiment

1845.   Greetham, William V., Captain 15th Hussars

1855.   Gregory, F. William, Captain 44th Regiment

1858.   Greig, Robert, Captain 61st Regiment

1852.   Greville, Arthur C., Major unattached

1860.   Greville, H. T. L., Captain Royal Artillery

1852.   Grey, Francis D., Major 63rd Regiment

1854.   Grierson, C., Major-General Royal Engineers

1838.   Griffith, H. Davies, late Cornet 22nd Lt. Drgs.

1859.   Griffith, John, late Assist.-Surg. 15th Hussars

O.M.   Grignon, James, late Captain 37th Regiment

1854.   Grimston, O. A., late Captain 19th Regiment

1859.   Grimston, R. V. S., Captain 49th Regiment

1858.   Grimston, W. G., Captain Royal Artillery

1848.   Grogan, Charles E., Captain 14th Regiment

1854.   Grove, James B., Lieutenant Royal Navy

1843.   Grove, T. F., late Captain 6th Dragoons

1855.   Grylls, Shadwell M., Major Royal Artillery

1851.   Gubbins, James, Major 23rd Fusiliers

1854.   Gubbins, Joseph, late Ensign 28th Regiment

O.M.   Gulliver, George, Surgeon H.P. R.H. Guards

1849.   Gunnell, Edmund H., Commander Royal Navy

1854.   Gunter, Robert, Captain 4th Dragoon Guards

1853.   Gwilt, John, Lieut.-Colonel 34th Regiment

H.

1856. Hackett, Samuel, Major unattached
1851. Hadden, William C., Colonel Royal Engineers
1838. Hadley, Henry, *M.D.*, Staff-Surgeon-Major
1842. Haffenden, A., late Lieutenant 8th Hussars
1852. Hale, Charles C., late Lieutenant Rifle Brigade
1846. Hale, Edward B., *C.B.*, Colonel 82nd Regiment
1839. Hale, H. G., late Lieutenant 7th Fusiliers
1854. Hale, J. R., Blagden, Colonel unattached
1858. Hale Mathew H., Captain 26th Regiment
1855. Hale, Robert, Captain 7th Hussars
1851. Halford, C. A. D., late Capt. 5th Dragoon Gds.
1848. Halkett, Fredk. J. C., late Capt. 71st Highlanders
1856. Hall, Basil S. de R., Lieutenant Royal Navy
1840. Hall, W. T., late Captain 6th Regiment
1851. Halliday, George E., Major 82nd Regiment
1848. Hallyburton, Lord J. F. G., *G.C.H.*, Rear Adm.
1850. Halton, Lancelot, Captain 16th Lancers
1840. Hamilton, A., late Captain 17th Lancers
1850. Hamilton, Alexander, Commander Royal Navy
1839. Hamilton, A. G. W., Lt.-Col. R. A. ret. full pay
1859. Hamilton, A. H. C., Captain Royal Artillery
1846. Hamilton, A. T., late Captain 71st Highlanders

1855.   Hamilton, C. M., Major 92nd Highlanders
1855.   Hamilton, Francis F., Captain 4th Regiment
1854.   Hamilton G. R., late Capt. 5th Dragoon Gds.
1839.   Hamilton, H., late Capt. 13th Light Dragoons
1839.   Hamilton, Henry M., Lt.-Colonel 12th Regt.
1851.   Hamilton, Hugh, late Capt. 1st Dragoon Gds.
1846.   Hamilton, John F. C.. Captain Royal Navy
1847.   Hamilton, Louis H., Major 87th Fusiliers
1854.   Hamilton, Thomas R., Captain 98th Regiment
1846.   Hamilton, W. F., late Lieut. 79th Highlanders
1853.   Hamley, E. Bruce, Lieut.-Col. Royal Artillery
1840.   Hamley, W. G., Lieut.-Col. Royal Engineers
1847.   Hammersley, Frederick, Major 14th Regiment
1839.   Hammond Wm. O., late Lieut. 17th Lancers
1841.   Hamond, P., late Captain 34th Regiment
1858.   Hand, Henry, Lieutenant Royal Navy
1858.   Hand, John S., Captain 82nd Regiment
1855.   Handcock, Hon. R., late Capt. 41st Regiment
1856.   Handcock, Hon. R., late Lieut. 48th Regiment
1858.   Handley, Henry E., late Lieut. 2nd Dragoons
1848.   Hankey, Augustus B., Major 83rd Regiment
1841.   Hankey, Frederick, late Lieut. 75th Regiment
1853.   Hanley, Dudley, *M.D.*, Staff-Surgeon
1853.   Harbord, Hon. Ralph, late Captain 71st Regt.
1854.   Hardie, G. K., *M.D.*, Surgeon 73rd Regiment
1843.   Harding, F. Pym, *C.B.*, Colonel 22nd Regiment
1853.   Hardinge, Henry, Lieut.-Col. Rifle Brigade

1853. Hardy, Edward, Commander Royal Navy
1850. Hardy, William, Major Depôt Battalion
1860. Harington, Richd. E. S., Capt. Rifle Brigade
1857. Harman, George Byng, Major unattached
1839. Harper, W. H., late Capt. 4th Dragoon Guards
1840. Harrison, Broadley, Lieut.-Col. 11th Hussars
1841. Harrison, J., Captain H.P. 4th Light Dragoons
1850. Harrisson, C. M., late Captain 79th Highlanders
1856. Hart, James C., late Captain 16th Lancers
1857. Hartopp, J. W. C., late Captain 17th Lancers
1857. Hartopp, William W., Capt. Royal Horse Gds.
1840. Harvey, Gillmore, Commander Royal Navy
1852. Harvey, John E., Captain 41st Regiment
1854. Harvey, Thomas, late Captain 69th Regiment
1855. Hastings, Francis W., Major Royal Artillery
1854. Hatfield, R. W., late Lieutenant 10th Hussars
1846. Haviland, R. H., late Captain 85th Lt. Infantry
1855. Hawes, George Harrington, Major 9th Regt.
1847. Hawker, H. S., Commander Royal Navy
1851. Hawkes, Henry, Lieutenant Royal Navy
1838. Hawkes, John B., late Capt. 3rd Light Dragoons
1852. Hawkes, J. Clifton, late Captain 66th Regt.
1858. Hawkesley, A. C. D., late Lieut. 2nd Life Gds.
1848. Hawkins, Alexander C., Major Royal Artillery
1850. Hawkins, Frank K., Commander Royal Navy
1852. Hawkins, S. Moore, Lieut.-Col. 97th Regiment
1848. Hawkins, T. S., Lieut.-Colonel unattached

1847. Hawley, Robert B., Lieut.-Col. 60th Rifles
1843. Haworth, E. C. A., late Captain 17th Lancers
1853. Hawthorn, Robert, Captain Royal Engineers
1838. Hay, David, Lieut.-Col, late 6th Dragoon Gds.
1860. Hay, H. H., late Captain 5th Dragoon Guards
1849. Hay, Lord John, *C.B.*, Captain Royal Navy
1847. Hay, R. B., late Ensign 93rd Highlanders
1854. Hay, Robert John, Captain Royal Artillery
1853. Hay, W. Drummond, Captain 72nd Highlanders
1851. Hayes, H. G., late Captain 46th Regiment
1851. Haythorne, Edmund, Colonel 1st Royals
1841. Head, Henry B., Capt. H.P. 2nd Dragoon Gds.
1853. Hearn, Charles Bush, Surgeon 1st Royals
O.M. Heath, Edwin, Paymaster half-pay 88th Regt.
1848. Heath, J. M., late Lieutenant 64th Regiment
1848. Heath, W. A. J., Commander Royal Navy
1849. Heathcote, Charles P., late Capt. 52nd Lt. Infy.
1860. Heberden, Henry, Captain Royal Artillery
1850. Hedley, John, late Lieutenant 60th Rifles
1845. Hedley, Robert, late Captain 62nd Regiment
1857. Hedley, George L., Captain 24th Regiment
1854. Helyar, E. G., late Lieutenant 14th Regiment
1859. Helyar, John W., Captain 16th Regiment
1846. Henderson, E. Y. W., Major Royal Engineers
O.M. Henderson, John, late Capt. 14th Lt. Dragoons
1852. Henderson, S. H., Commander Royal Navy
O.M. Henderson, William, Colonel Royal Artillery

1855.	Heneage, A. C. F., Lieutenant Royal Navy
1855.	Henley, Arthur, Captain 52nd Lt. Infantry
1855.	Henning, Shurlock, Major 88th Regiment
1852.	Henry, Robert J., late Capt. 4th Dragoon Gds.
1850.	Herbert, Arthur J., Lieut.-Col. unattached
1851.	Herbert, M. F., late Captain 48th Regiment
1842.	Herbert, R. W. H., Lieutenant Royal Navy
1838.	Heriot, J., *M.D.*, Surgeon H.P. 6th Drg. Gds.
1854.	Herries, Frederick S., Captain 65th Regiment
1846.	Heywood, Thomas, late Captain 16th Lancers
1850.	Hibbert, Edward G., Major 12th Regiment
1847.	Hibbert, F. D., late Lieutenant 2nd Dragoons
1858.	Hibbert, Francis G., Capt. R. Canadian Rifles
1850.	Hibbert, Hugh R., Major 7th Fusiliers
1849.	Hibbert, Lester, late Lieutenant 1st Royals
1859.	Hickes, Henry J. F. E., Capt. Royal Artillery
1840.	Hickey, Edward, Lieut.-Col., late 69th Regt.
1858.	Higgon, John D. G., Captain Royal Artillery
1855.	Hill, Charles R., Capt. Royal Artillery
1848.	Hill, Dudley Clarges, Captain 40th Regiment
O.M.	Hill, Edward, Major, late 96th Regiment
1859.	Hill, Francis C., Captain 56th Regiment
O.M.	Hill, Percy, *C.B.*, Colonel Rifle Brigade
1859.	Hill, Peter Edward, Captain Royal Artillery
O.M.	Hill, Stephen J., *C.B.*, Col., late 3rd Lt. Drgs.
1859.	Hill, Thomas, Captain 11th Regiment
1838.	Hill, Hon. W. N., Col. late 13th Lt. Infantry

1848.   Hilliard, George, late Captain 18th Regiment

1840.   Hilton, Thomas, late Captain 19th Regiment

1846.   Hinde, Edwin T., Commander Royal Navy

1852.   Hinxman, Rowley W., Captain 60th Rifles

1851.   Hives, Alfred, late Lieutenant 9th Lancers

1846.   Hoare, M. E., late Lieutenant 15th Hussars

1847.   Hoare, W. O'B., Commander Royal Navy

1845.   Hobart, Hon. A. C., Commander Royal Navy

1851.   Hobson, Samuel, late Captain 10th Regiment

1844.   Hobson, S. Le Hunt, late Lieut. 37th Regt.

1850.   Hodgson, Wm. C., Lt.-Col. 79th Highlanders

1847.   Hogge, Cameron N., Lt.-Colonel Grenadier Gds.

1848.   Hogge, J. Swaine, Major 5th Fusiliers

1859.   Hogge, Somerville G. C., Captain 16th Regt.

1860.   Hohenlohe-Lagenberg, His Serene Highness Prince Victor of, Captain Royal Navy

1849.   Holder, Chas., late Lt.-Col. Scots Fusilier Gds.

1843.   Holden, Henry, Lt.-Col., late 13th Lt. Dragoons

1848.   Holdich, E. A., *C.B.*, Colonel 20th Regiment

1838.   Hole, Alfred R., late Cornet 13th Lt. Dragoons

1845.   Holmes, Robert C., late Captain 10th Hussars

1843.   Holworthy, Edw. J., Major 14th Regiment

O.M.   Home, Rodham C. D., late Lieut. 67th Regt.

1847.   Home, W., *M.D.*, Staff-Surgeon-Major

1850.   Hood, Arthur W. A., Captain Royal Navy

1847.   Hood, Charles, Lt.-Col. 58th Regiment

1855.   Hookey, James, Lieutenant Royal Navy

1850. Hope, Charles W., Commander Royal Navy
1858. Hope, J. Edward, Major Royal Artillery
1860. Hope, William, *V. C.*, late Lieut. 7th Fusiliers
1855. Hopetoun, John, Earl of, late Lt. 1st Life Gds.
1852. Hopson, F. T., Paymaster 3rd Light Dragoons
1847. Hopson, William H., Major, late 26th Regiment
1845. Hore, Edward G., Captain Royal Navy
1853. Hore, T., Major-General Royal Engineers
1845. Hornby, Geoffrey T. P., Captain Royal Navy
1838. Hornby, Thomas W., late Capt. 82nd Regiment
1858. Hornby, Robert M., Captain Military Train
1859. Horne, Edward G., Captain 25th Regiment
O.M. Horne, George, Captain 12th Lancers
1846. Horne, James, late Captain 92nd Highlanders
1856. Horne, William H., Captain 2nd Dragoon Gds.
1848. Hort, John J., Lieut.-Colonel 36th Regiment
1851. Hoskins, Anthony H., Commander Royal Navy
1847. Hotham, Augustus T., late Capt. 75th Regiment
1852. Howard, R. Graham, late Lieut. 45th Regiment
O.M. Howarth, Richard, Lieut.-Col. Royal Engineers
1851. Hozier, W. W., late Lieutenant 2nd Dragoons
O.M. Huband, George J., late Captain 8th Hussars
1840. Hudson, Thomas W., Lieut.-Colonel unattached
1856. Hughes, C. J., Captain 51st Light Infantry
1840. Hughes, J. W. M. G., late Lieut. 13th Lt. Drgs.
1854. Hughes, R. G., Major-General retired full-pay
1849. Hughes, R. J., Captain & Adjt. Dep. Battalion

F

1838. Hughes, Wm. J. M., late Capt. 1st Drg. Gds.
1852. Hull, William, late Lieut. Coldstream Guards
O.M. Hulse, R. S., late Capt. Coldstream Guards
O.M. Humbley, William W. W., Captain unattached
1844. Hume, Gustavus, Major unattached
1855. Hume, G. P., Lt.-Colonel, late 15th Regiment
1842. Hume, Henry, *C.B.*, Colonel Grenadier Guards
1852. Hume John Richard, Captain 55th Regiment
1852. Hume, Robert, Lieutenant-Col. 55th Regiment
1841. Hume, T. D., *M.D.*, Dep. Inspector-General
1847. Humphreys, W. H., Capt. R. Can. Rifle Regt.
1850. Hunt, Augustus, late Captain 6th Dragoons
1850. Hunt, E. D'Arcy, Major 6th Dragoons
1859. Hunter, C. Fleming, Captain 72nd Regiment
1855. Hunter, John, Captain 17th Regiment
1855. Hunter, Robert, S., Capt. 6th Dragoon Guards
1852. Hunter, T., *M.D.*, Deputy-Inspector-General
1853. Hutchinson, C. S., Lt.-Col. 2nd Dragoon Gds.
1850. Hutchinson, Sir E. S., Bart., late Lt. 48th Regt.
1859. Hutchison, Fred. J., Captain 64th Regiment
1860. Hutton, G. M., late Lieut. 46th Regiment
1853. Hutton, Thomas, Major late 4th Light Dragoons
O.M. Hyde, G. H., Col. Rl. Artillery retired full-pay

I.

1849. Ibbetson, J. K., late Lieut. 14th Light Dragoons
1857. Ibbetson, Charles P., Lieut.-Colonel unattached
O.M. Ince, Ralph P., Major, late Rifle Brigade
O.M. Ingham, Chas. T., *M.D.*, Surg. H.P. 54th Regt.
1858. Ingham, C. D., Captain 28th Regiment
1859. Ingham, Joshua C., Captain 36th Regiment
1851. Inglis, John, late Captain 11th Hussars
1838. Inglis, Sir J. Eardley W., *K.C.B.*, Maj.-General
        Colonel 32nd Light Infantry
1846. Inglis, Raymond, Major, late 7th Fusiliers
1839. Inglis, Thomas C., late Captain Rifle Brigade
1845. Inglis, William, Lieut-Colonel 57th Regiment
1851. Inglis, William, Major, late 5th Dragoon Gds.
1853. Ingram, H. F. W., Commander Royal Navy
1843. Innes, Norman M., late Lieut. 17th Lancers
1841. Innes, W. S. Mitchell, late Lieut. 16th Lancers
1841. Ireland, R. P., Captain 3rd W. I. Regiment
1855. Irvine, Edward T., late Captain 16th Lancers
1855. Irving, Robert N., late Lieut. 12th Regiment
O.M. Isacke, Fredericke J., late Capt. 89th Regiment
1860. Ives, Gordon M., late Lieut. Coldstream Gds.

J.

1839. Jackson, George W. C., Major late 7th Hussars
1855. Jackson, Standish R., Lieut. 78th Regiment
1846. Jackson, William T. F., Lieutenant Royal Navy
1838. Jacob, Geo. T., late Capt. 4th Dragoon Guards
1852. James, Charles, Lieut.-Col. late 2nd Regiment
1850. James, D. W. Grevis, Major 2nd Regiment
1856. James, Edward R., Captain Royal Engineers
1855. James, Henry, late Captain 20th Regiment
O.M. James, Sir John K., late Lieut. 6th Dragoons
1851. Jameson, Robert O'B., late Capt. 11th Hussars
1854. Jarvis, Samuel P., Major half-pay 82nd Regiment
1839. Jauncey, H. J., late Captain 62nd Regiment
1847. Jee, Joseph, *C.B.*, *V.C.*, Surg. 78th Highlanders
O.M. Jefferson, Richard, Lt. H.P. Ceylon Rifle Regt.
1847. Jenings, George B., Major 19th Regiment
1840. Jenkinson, Sir G. S., Bart. late Capt. 8th Hussars
1838. Jenner, Augustus F., Lt.-Col. 11th Regiment
1849. Jenner, R. F. L., late Captain 7th Fusiliers
1849. Jenyns, Soame G., *C.B.*, Major 18th Hussars
1854. Jervis, Edw. Lennox, Major 6th Dragoon Gds.
1857. Jervois, E. Stanhope, Capt. H.P. 7th Fusiliers
1854. Jervoise, Henry Clarke, Capt. Coldstream Gds.

1858. Jex, Blake R. Hoey, Captain 18th Regiment
O.M. Jocelyn, Hon. A G. F., Major, late 6th Drg. Gds.
1855. Johns, Thomas, late Captain 63rd Regiment
1857. Johnson, Alured C., Major Royal Artillery
1846. Johnson, Chardin P., Major 9th Lancers
1847. Johnson, G. V., Major Royal Artillery
1843. Johnson, Sir H. F., Bt., Lt.-Col. H.P. 5th Fus.
1849. Johnson, William V., late Capt. 90th Lt. Infy.
1839. Johnston, Patrick, Captain unattached
O.M. Johnston, Thomas H., Major-General
1855. Johnstone, Charles, Captain Royal Artillery
1851. Johnstone, Robert B., Captain 45th Regiment
1858. Johnstone, C. J. H., Captain Royal Artillery
1851. Jolliffe, H. H., *M.P.*, late Capt. Coldstream Gds.
1849. Jones, Arthur, Paymaster Royal Navy
1847. Jones, Douglas, Major half-pay 60th Rifles
1855. Jones, Hastings F., late Lieutenant 1st Royals
1858. Jones, Hugh M., Major 73rd Regiment
1848. Jones, J. C., late Captain 2nd Dragoon Guards
1852. Jones, J. Inglis, late Lieut. Royal Horse Guards
1841. Jones, Oliver John, Captain Royal Navy
1846. Jones, Thomas, Major 4th Dragoon Guards
1846. Jopp, James, *M.D.*, Surgeon-Major 36th Regt.
1853. Jordan, Joseph, Major 34th Regiment
1856. Jortin, Henry Lee-, late Lieut. 2nd Life Guards
1846. Judd, W. H., Surg.-Major H.P. Scots Fus. Gds.

K.

O.M.   Keane, George M., Lt.-Col., late 2nd Regiment
1852.   Keane, Giles, Colonel 86th Regt. ret. full pay
1841.   Keane, Hon. G. D., Captain Royal Navy
1839.   Keane, Hon. Hussey F., Major Royal Engineers
1840.   Keane, Hon. J. A., late Captain Rifle Brigade
1855.   Keate, Edward, Captain Royal Artillery
1845.   Keene, E. Ruck-, Major late 2nd Drg. Grds.
1855.   Keene, George Ruck-, Lieutenant Royal Navy
1858.   Keene, J. E. Ruck-, Captain Royal Artillery
1843.   Kellett, Henry, C.B., Captain Royal Navy
1846.   Kendall, Henry, MD., Surgeon 7th Hussars
1847.   Kennedy, Francis, late Captain 77th Regiment
1854.   Kennedy, F. C., Captain 25th Regiment
1850.   Kennedy, J. J., C.B., Captain Royal Navy
1853.   Kennedy, J. S., late Lieutenant 36th Regiment
1843.   Kennedy, Lord William, late Capt. R. Artillery
1858.   Kent, Henry, Major 77th Regiment
1840.   Keown, Henry, late Captain 15th Hussars
1850.   Kerin, Fredk. G., Surgeon 2nd Life Guards
1840.   Kerr, Lord Mark, C.B., Col. 13th Lt Infantry
1857.   Kerr, Robert D., late Captain Royal Engineers
1852.   Kerr, William H., Major 13th Light Infantry

1838.	Key, Charles H., late Capt. 2nd Dragoon Gds.
1847.	Key, George William, Colonel H.P. 44th Regt.
1853.	Kidd, Robert Charles, late Lieut. 9th Lancers
1855.	King, Augustus H., Captain R. H. Artillery
1853.	King, E. Raleigh late Capt. 13th Lt. Dragoons
1852.	King, Edward T., late Lieutenant 21st Fusiliers
1847.	King, John Hynde, Lieut.-Col. Grenadier Gds.
1847.	King, J. Henry, Captain & Paymaster 2nd Drgs.
1860.	King, Isaac, Lieutenant 41st Regiment
1854.	King, William A., Captain 17th Regiment
1855.	King, William Ross, Major unattached
1858.	King, William W., Captain 12th Lancers
1844.	Kingston, Arthur B., Lieutenant Royal Navy
1842.	Kirby, William H., Lieut.-Col. 94th Regiment
1848.	Kirkwall, G. W., Viscount, late Captain Scots Fusilier Guards
1858.	Knatchbull, Francis, Captain 89th Regiment
1854.	Knatchbull, W., late Captain 3rd Dragoon Gds.
1850.	Knight, Arnold M., Captain 12th Regiment
O.M.	Knight, Brook J., Capt. H.P. Royal Staff Corps
1843.	Knight, C. R., late Captain 25th Regiment
1846.	Knight, E. L., late Captain 20th Regiment
1853.	Knight, Lewis E., Major 17th Lancers
1848.	Knight, W. W., late Lieutenant Rifle Brigade
1857.	Knipe, William, Captain 86th Regiment
1854.	Knox, Henry N., Lieutenant Royal Navy
O.M.	Knox, Richard, Lieut.-Colonel 18th Hussars

1838.   Knox, Thomas Edmond, Lieut.-Col. 67th Regt.
1844.   Knox, Hon. W. S., *M.P.*, Maj. late 21st Fusiliers
1846.   Kortright, Augustus, late Ensign 68th Lt. Inf.
1844.   Kortright, William C., late Lieut. 9th Lancers

L.

O.M.	Labalmondiere, D. W. P., Capt. H.P. 45th Regt.
O.M.	Lacy, Thomas E., Colonel unattached
1849.	Laffan, Robert M., Lt.-Col. Royal Engineers
O.M.	Laidley, John, Commissary-General half-pay
1844.	Lalor, E. J. Power, late Capt. 1st Dragoon Gds.
1850.	Lamb, George H., late Capt. 49th Regiment
1851.	Lamb, W. W., Captain 7th Dragoon Guards
1853.	Lambert, E. H. G., Commander Royal Navy
1850.	Lambert, Thomas, late Captain Royal Artillery
1858.	Lambert, W. M., late Captain 41st Regiment
1857.	Lance, W. H. J., Lieutenant 98th Regiment
1850.	Lane, Douglas, late Captain 17th Lancers
1848.	Lane, Ernest H., late Capt. 4th Dragoon Gds.
1855.	Lane, Henry C., late Lieut. 2nd Life Guards
1843.	Lang, Edward W., Captain Royal Navy
1839.	Lang, Frederick H., late Capt. 34th Regiment
1852.	Langley, George R., Captain unattached
1852.	Langley, W. L., *M.D.*, Staff-Surgeon-Major
1853.	Lascelles, Claud G., Captain Royal Artillery
1856.	Lascelles, Hon. H. D., Lieutenant Royal Navy
1858.	Laurie, John W., Captain 4th Regiment
1854.	Latouche, O., late Captain 14th Regiment

1840. Law, Charles E., Colonel 66th Regiment
1858. Lawrence, Henry J. H. Assis, Surg. Gren. Gds.
1846. Lawrenson, John, Major-General
1846. Lawrie, John, Major, late Depôt Battalion
1849. Lawson, J. H., late Lieut. 3rd Dragoon Guards
1852. Layton, Charles Miller, late Capt. 25th Regt.
1854. Leader, Henry E., late Captain 16th Lancers
1854. Learmonth, Alex., Lt.-Col., late 17th Lancers
1843. Le Blanc, Thomas E., late Capt. 37th Regiment
1845. Lee, Henry, Major 15th Hussars
1854. Lee, Ranulph C., Captain 35th Regiment
1859. Lee, Vaughn H., Captain 21st Regiment
1852. Legge, Hon. & Rev. G. B.,late Capt. R. Brigade
1854. Legh W. John, late Captain 21st Fusiliers
1851. Legrew, John.Vet. Surg. 2nd Life Gds., 1st class
1838. Leigh, Egerton, late Capt. 2nd Dragoon Guards
1855. Le Marchant, Edward, Capt. H.P. 57th Regt.
1851. Le Mesurier, W., Deputy-Commissary-General
1860. Leiningen, His Serene Highness The Prince
       of, Commander Royal Navy
1856. Leith, Sir G. H., Bart., late Capt. 17th Lancers
1847. Lennox, Augustus F. F., Major Royal Artillery
1850. Lennox, W. Oates, *V.C.*, Lt.-Col. R. Engineers
1844. Leslie, Arthur, Lieut.-Colonel 40th Regiment
1847. Leslie, George, Captain Royal Artillery
1843. Leslie, Lewis X., Major, late 99th Regiment
1858. L'Estrange, P. W., Major Royal Artillery

1856.   Lethbridge, W. A., late Lieut. Rifle Brigade
1856.   Levett, Edward, Major 10th Hussars
O.M.   Levett, Richard B., late Lieutenant 60th Rifles
1838.   Levett, Theophilus, late Capt. 11th Hussars
1851.   Levinge, Charles H., Captain 93rd Regiment
O.M.   Levinge, Sir R. G. A., Bt., late Capt. 5th Drg. Gds.
1855.   Lewins, Robert, *M.D.*, Staff-Surgeon
1844.   Lewis, J. Edward, Lieut.-Colonel unattached
1845.   Ley, James, late Captain 2nd Dragoon Guards
1855.   Liddell, Hon. Atholl C. J., Capt. 60th Rifles
1850.   Lightfoot, Thomas, *C.B.*, Lt.-Col. 84th Regt.
1853.   Lillie, Thos., Lt.-Col., late Ceylon Rifle Regt.
1848.   Lindow, C. T., late Lieut. 6th Dragoon Guards
1844.   Lindow, H. W., late Lieutenant 17th Lancers
1842.   Lindsay, Alexander C., late Capt. 44th Regt.
1849.   Lindsay, Henry Gore, late Capt. Rifle Brigade
O.M.   Lindsay, John, late Lieut. 2nd Life Guards
1855.   Linton, William, *M.D.*, *C.B.*, Insp. General
1848.   Lister, Frederick D., Lieut.-Col., late 6th Drgs.
O.M.   Little, Archibald, *C.B.*, Colonel 9th Lancers
1840.   Little, Lockhart, late Captain 81st Regiment
1849.   Littledale, Edward, Major, late 1st Dragoons
1847.   Littledale, G. H., late Lieutenant 1st Dragoons
1852.   Lloyd, Edward, Captain 6th Regiment
O.M.   Lloyd, Evan H., late Captain 1st Dragoons
1846.   Lloyd, Rickard, Captain 36th Regiment
1859.   Lloyd, Thomas, Lieutenant 35th Regiment

O.M. Lloyd, W., *M.D.*, Surgeon half-pay 36th Regt.

1854. Lluellyn, Richard, late Captain 46th Regiment

1858. Lluellyn, W. R., Captain Royal Artillery

1847. Loder, W. S., late Lieutenant 63rd Regiment

1847. Loftus, Arthur J., late Captain 18th Hussars

1847. Logan, T. G., *M.D.*, Inspector-General

1851. Loney, W., *M.D.*, Surgeon Royal Navy

1838. Long, John, late Lieutenant 10th Hussars

1840. Lord, A. O., late Captain 72nd Highlanders

1847. Lousada, Simeon C., late Capt. 18th Regiment

1858. Lovell, N. de Jersey, Captain 6th Dragoons

1842. Low, Alexander, Colonel unattached

1859. Lowe, Drury Curzon, Captain 17th Lancers

1841. Lowe, Edward W.D., *C.B.*, Lt.-Col. 21st Regt.

1839. Lowndes, H. W. S., late Captain 15th Hussars

1839. Lucas, Richard, late Lieut. 2nd Life Guards

1855. Luce, John Proctor, Captain Royal Navy

1857. Lukin, Fredk. W., Paymaster 2nd Drg. Gds.

1850. Lukin, W. W. A., Major Royal Artillery

O.M. Lumley, Frederick D., Lieut.-Col. unattached

1854. Lutyens, Charles, late Captain 20th Regiment

1859. Lyle, Hugh C., Captain Royal Artillery

1854. Lynch, William W., Captain 2nd Regiment

1850. Lyon, C. J., late Ensign 52nd Light Infantry

1849. Lyon, Edmund D., late Capt. 68th Lt. Infantry

1855. Lyon, Francis, Captain Royal Horse Artillery

1856. Lyon, F. L., Captain Royal Artillery

1849. Lyon, H. D. W., Captain 2nd Life Guards
1851. Lyon, T. H., late Lieutenant Royal Navy
1860. Lyons, Algernon M., Commander Royal Navy
1855. Lyons, James, Captain Royal Artillery
1852. Lyons, Thomas C., Major 20th Regiment
O.M. Lysaght, James R., late Lieut. 84th Regiment
1841. Lysaght, Thomas, H., Commander Royal Navy
O.M. Lysons, Daniel, *C.B.*, Colonel unattached

M.

1855.	Macartney, G. T., late Captain 15th Hussars
1841.	Macartney, John. Captain 17th Lancers
1844.	Macartney. J. N., Major late 7th Dragoon Gds.
1858.	Macbeth, James, *M.D.*, Surgeon 74th Regt.
1858.	Macdonald, George V., late Captain 19th Regt.
1855.	Macdonell, Alex., *C.B.*, Colonel Rifle Brigade
1846.	Macdonell, John I., Captain 71st Highlanders
1842.	MacDonell, John, Captain Royal Navy
O.M.	MacDougall, Patrick L., Colonel Commandant Royal Staff College
1855.	Mac Farlan, J. W., Captain Military Train
1845.	Mac Farlane, F. J., Captain 3rd Dragoon Gds.
1858.	Mac Henry, John, late Captain 77th Regiment
1855.	Mackenzie, J. K. D., Captain 86th Regiment
O.M.	Mackinnon, Daniel H., Major unattached
O.M.	Mackinnon, D. H. A., late Capt. 68th Lt. Inf.
1838.	Mackinnon, E. V., Paym. H.P. 5th Drg. Gds.
1852.	Maclean, A. Capt. & Staff Officer of Pensioners
1856.	Maclean, Fitzroy D., Captain 13th Lt. Dragoons
1839.	Maclean, Sir G., *K.C.B.*, Commissary-General
1847.	Maclean, Henry J., Captain Rifle Brigade
1855.	Macleod, Robert B. Æ., Lieutenant Royal Navy

1843. Mac Mahon, William, Lieut.-Col. 44th Regt.
1850. Macneill, Robert, Captain 13th Light Dragoons
1856. Macpherson, A. J., Major 24th Regiment
1858. Macpherson, Eneas M., Staff-Surgeon
1856. Macqueen, M. P., late Captain 91st Regiment
1857. McBarnet, Alex. C., Major 79th Highlanders
O.M. McCall, George, late Captain 20th Regiment
1853. McCall, William, Lieut.-Colonel unattached
1851. McClintock, T. M., late Captain 91st Regiment
1854. McCourt, John, Major Military Train
1847. McCreagh, Michael, Capt. 4th Dragoon Guards
1853. McDonnell, F., late Ensign 71st Highlanders
1845. McDonnell, John, Capt. Cape Mounted Rifles
1847. McEvoy, E., *M.P.*, late Lieut, 6th Dragoon Grds.
1854. MccGwire, E. T. St. L., Captain 1st Royals
O.M. McKerlie, John G., Lt.-Col. Royal Engineers
1852. McNeile, Henry H., late Lieut. 5th Drg. Gds.
1858. McNeill, Duncan, Captain 2nd Dragoons
1851. McNeill, W. H., late Captain 20th Regiment
1855. McWhinnie, John, *M.D.*, Surgeon Royal Navy
1858. Madden, Samuel A., Captain 51st Regiment
1838. Madocks, J., late Captain 13th Light Dragoons
1858. Magnay, C. James, Captain 16th Regiment
1841. Mahon, H. S. P., late Lieutenant 8th Hussars
O.M. Mahony, M., *M.D.*, Inspector-General
1839. Mainwaring, Arthur, late Capt. 66th Regiment
1840. Mainwaring, Rowland, Rear-Admiral

1839.	Malassez, C. T., Assistant Commissary-General
1850.	Mallett, Hugh, late Lieutenant 9th Lancers
1855.	Manders, Richard, late Lieut. 15th Regiment
1847.	Manley, Robert G., Major, late 6th Dragoons
1848.	Mann, John B., Lieutenant-Colonel unattached
1845.	Manners, H. Russell, Major Depôt Battalion
1853.	Mansel, Arthur E.; Capt. 3rd Light Dragoons
O.M.	Mansel, Herbert, late Lieutenant 61st Regiment
1850.	Mansfield, Charles, E., Major unattached
O.M.	Mansfield, Sir William R., *K.C.B*,, Major-Gen.
1848.	Mapleton, Henry, *M.D.*, Deputy Insp.-General
1849.	March, W. H., Lt.-Col. R. Marines Lt. Infantry
1848.	Margesson, W. G., Captain 56th Regiment
1853.	Markham, E., Captain Royal Horse Artillery
1850.	Markham, Wm. T., late Capt. Coldstream Gds.
1842.	Marriott, T. B. F., Colonel Royal Artillery
1853.	Marsh, A, Leacock, Major, late 55th Regiment
1859.	Marsh, Henry Dyke, Lieut. 82nd Regiment
1846.	Marsh, Sir Henry, Bart., Major 3rd Drg. Grds.
1854.	Marshall, Edward, Captain Royal Navy
1852.	Marshall, Frederick, Captain 2nd Life Guards
1849.	Marston, Henry F., Captain 9th Regiment
1855.	Martin, Cornwallis W., Lieutenant Royal Navy
1857.	Martin, George P., Paymaster Royal Navy
O.M.	Martyn, Peter, late Captain 88th Regiment
1854.	Mason, James, late Captain 94th Regiment
1853.	Massey, Hon. E. C , Lt.-Col. 95th Regiment

1851.   Massy, Godfrey W. H., Major unattached

1856.   Massy, Hugh, Major, late 85th Light Infantry

1845.   Massy, H. H. J., late Captain 44th Regiment

1858.   Master, W. C., *C.B.*, Lieut.-Col. 5th Fusiliers

1840.   Mathison, Charles M., Captain Royal Navy

1851.   Maude, Francis C., *C.B.*, Lt.-Col. R. Artillery

1856.   Maude, Fredk. F., *C.B.,V.C.*, Lt.-Col. 3rd Buffs

1858.   Maunsell, C. Cullen, late Captain 54th Regiment

1856.   Maunsell, Edward E., Lieutenant Royal Navy

1853.   Maunsell, T. E., late Captain 12th Lancers

1846.   Maunsell, W. W., late Captain 66th Regiment

1843.   Maxwell, Edward H., Lieut.-Col. 88th Regt.

1851.   Maxwell, George S., late Lieut. 20th Regiment

1846.   Maxwell, G. Vaughan, *C.B.*, Colonel 88th Regt.

1839.   Maxwell, Hon. J. P., *M.P.*, Lt.-Col. late 97th Rgt.

1859.   Maxwell, Robert James, Captain 80th Regiment

1842.   Maycock, Dottin, late Lieutenant 6th Dragoons

1846.   Maycock, John G. Captain 14th Regiment

1839.   Maydwell, Henry L., Lieut.-Colonel Staff

1840.   Mayers, John Perkins, Lt.-Col., late 86th Regt.

1853.   Mayne, Taylor L., Major unattached

1844.   Mayo, John P., late Lieut. 74th Highlanders

O.M.   Meade, John, late Captain 43rd Light Infantry

1852.   Meade, R. Richard, Captain 8th Regiment

1858.   Meara, Edward S., Lieutenant Royal Navy

1858.   Meara, William, H.P. Major 5th Fusiliers

1856.   Mecham, Maunsell, late Lieut. 92nd Highlanders

1849.   Mein, Frederick R., Major 1st Royals

1851.   Meredyth, H. W., late Lieut. 68th Lt. Infantry

O.M.   Meyer, L. C. A., Lieut.-Col. late Cavalry Depôt

1839.   Meynell, Francis, late Capt. 2nd Dragoon Gds.

O.M.   Michel, Charles E., Major-General

1850.   Michell, John E., Lieut.-Colonel Royal Artillery

1858.   Micklethwaite, George N., late Capt. 44th Regt.

1850.   Middleton, Frederick D., Major 29th Regiment

O.M.   Middleton, John, Major, Paymaster half-pay

O.M.   Middleton, T. F., Lieut. H.P. 1st Dragoons Gds.

1843.   Middleton, W. A., *C.B.*, Lt.-Col. Royal Artillery

1854.   Mildmay, H.G.St.John, Commander Royal Navy.

1844.   Miles, Charles W., late Captain 17th Lancers

1846.   Miles, Philip J. W., late Lieut. 17th Lancers

O.M.   Miller, A. P., late Captain 92nd Highlanders

1854.   Miller, D. S., late Captain 7th Fusiliers

1859.   Miller, Frederick, Major 80th Regiment

1846.   Miller G. Murray, Major 79th Highlanders

1851.   Miller, James Armit, Surgeon Royal Navy.

1843.   Miller, James Boyd, late Captain 15th Hussars

1851.   Miller, Robert B., Commander Royal Navy

O.M.   Miller, Sir W., Bart., late Lieut. 12th Lancers

1854.   Milles, Hon. L. W., Major Rifle Brigade

1858.   Millett, Sydney C., Captain 23rd Fusiliers.

1858.   Milligan, Charles, Captain 39th Regiment

1854.   Milman, E. C. W., Colonel 37th Regiment

1842.   Milman, G. Bryan, Lieut.-Colonel 5th Fusiliers

1843. Milman, G. H. L., Major Royal Artillery
1857. Milman, W. D., Captain Royal Artillery .
1858. Milner, Wm. S., late Captain 10th Regiment
1851. Mitchell, Alfred, Commander Royal Navy.
1853. Mitchell, T. J., Captain 1st Dragoon Guards
1854. Mitford, H. R., late Captain 51st Light Infantry
1843. Mitford, J. P., Major, late 2nd W. I. Regiment
1853. Mockler, Edward, Staff-Surgeon-Major
1843. Mollan, William C., *C.B.*, Lt.-Col. 75th Regt.
1845. Molyneux, Charles B., late Capt. 4th Lt. Drgs.
1838. Monro, Alexander, late Captain Rifle Brigade
1850. Monro, C. J. Hale, late Captain 36th Regiment
1839. Monro, David Arthur, Major, late 12th Lancers
1849. Monro, Hector, late Captain 57th Regiment
1845. Monro, J., *M.D.*, Surg.-Major Coldstream Gds.
1856. Monro, W., late Captain 79th Highlanders
1858. Monson, Hon. D. J., Captain 52nd Lt. Infantry
1848. Montagu, J. Van H., Captain 10th Regiment
1852. Montgomerie, Frederick, late Capt. 99th Regt.
1855. Montgomerie, J. E., Commander Royal Navy
O.M. Montgomery, Francis O., Major, late 45th Regt.
1849. Montgomery Henry, late Capt. 42nd Highlanders
1852. Montgomery, Hugh P., Captain 60th Rifles
1854. Montgomery, R. J., Captain 5th Dragoon Guards
1847. Montresor, E. J. T., late Capt. 55th Regiment
1849. Montresor, John, late Captain 82nd Regiment
1840. Moor, Frederick, late Lieutenant 2nd Regiment

1854. Moore, A. G. M., Captain 4th Light Dragoons
1855. Moore, Edward, Lieut.-Colonel 11th Regiment
1859. Moore, Henry, Assistant Commissary-General
1855. Moore, T. C. C., Colonel, Second Commandant
   Royal Marines Light Infantry
1847. Morant, Edward, Major, late 12th Lancers
1845. Morant, Horatio H., Major 68th Light Infantry
1859. Moresby, M. F., Paymaster Royal Navy
1852. Moreton, Hon. A. T., late Capt. 3rd Lt. Drgs.
1851. Morgan, Hon.G.Chas.,*M.P.*,late Capt. 17thLan.
1853. Morgan, G. M., late Capt. 4th Dragoon Guards
1841. Morgan, Herbert, late Captain 1st Dragoons
1847. Morgan, H. C., late Lieut. 1st Dragoon Guards
1858. Morgan, Hon. Fred. C., late Capt. Rifle Brigade
1844. Morris, C. H., *C.B.*, Lieut.-Col. unattached
1850. Morris, Frederick, Lieutenant Royal Navy
1853. Morris, Herbert, Captain 80th Regiment
1844. Morritt, R. A., late Lieutenant 77th Regiment
1846. Morshead, Sir W. C., Bart., late Capt. 6th Drgs.
1838. Mosley Tonman, late Lieutenant 6th Dragoons
1859. Mostyn, Hon. Roger, Lt.-Col. Scots Fus. Gds.
1859. Mostyn, Hon. Savage, Captain 23rd Fusiliers
1858. Mounsey, Charles James, Capt. 71st Regiment
1846. Mount-Charles,G.H., Earl of, Capt.1st Life Gds
O.M. Moysey, H. Gorges, late Lieut. 11th Hussars
1854. Mundy, George Rodney, *C.B.*, Rear-Admiral
1852. Mundy, Meynell H. M., Lieutenant Royal Navy

1839.   Mundy, P. Henry, Colonel Royal Artillery

O.M.   Mundy, R. M., Major, half-pay Royal Artillery

1860.   Munn, H. O., Captain 13th Light Dragoons

1850.   Munnings, William V., Captain 24th Regiment

1841.   Munro, J. St. John, Major, late 31st Regiment

1838.   Munro, Sir Thos., Bart., late Capt. 10th Hussars

1858.   Mure, Charles R., Captain 43rd Regiment

1849.   Mure, John, *M.D.*, Staff-Surgeon-Major

1858.   Murphy, Jacob C., Captain 7th Dragoon Gds.

1843.   Murray, Alexander, Colonel 87th Fusiliers

1846.   Murray, Augustus G. E., Lieutenant Royal Navy

1842.   Murray, Henry, late Capt. 79th Highlanders

1838.   Murray, Hon. Henry A., Captain Royal Navy

1842.   Murray, Jack H., Commander Royal Navy

1854.   Murray, John, Captain 94th Regiment

1839.   Murray, William, Major, late 12th Lancers

1855.   Musgrave, Philip, late Lieutenant 17th Lancers

1858.   Mussenden, William, Captain 8th Hussars

1858.   Muttlebury, Geo. A., late Lieut. 4th Drg. Guards

N.

1846. Nairne, J. Mellis, late Captain 38th Regiment
1858. Nangle, Henry, Captain 15th Regiment ·
1848. Napier, Edward P., late Lieut. 59th Regiment
1848. Napier, G. T. C., *C.B.*, Colonel unattached
1839. Napier, Sir R. J., Milliken, Bt., late Capt. 79th Regt.
1838. Napier, William C. E., Colonel unattached
1841. Naylor, James Sadler, Lt.-Col. late 8th Hussars
1856. Neave, Arundell, Captain 3rd Dragoon Guards
1846. Need, Arthur, Major 14th Light Dragoons
1841. Nelson, Alexander A., Major unattached
1849. Nelson, Horatio, Commander Royal Navy
1841. Nelson, Thomas L. K., Major 40th Regiment
1852. Nevill, George Henry, late Capt. 7th Fusiliers
1854. Nevill, Percy P., Lt.-Col. late Major 63rd Regt.
1848. Newdigate, Edward, Major Rifle Brigade
1855. Newdigate, Henry R. L., Major Rifle Brigade
1854. Newenham, W. H., late Captain 63rd Regiment
1854. Newland, Arthur, late Captain 1st Royals
1838. Newland, B., late Captain 1st Dragoon Guards
1848. Newman, Sir Lydston, Bart., late Capt. 7th Huss.
1844. Newton, Horace P., Major Royal Horse Artillery
1859. Nicholas, Griffin, Major 5th Fus., ret. full pay

1858.   Nicholl, Hume, Captain 1st Dragoons

1849.   Nicholson, Lothian, *C.B.*, Lt.-Col. R. Engineers

O.M.   Nicoll, Samuel J. L., Lt.-Col., late 30th Regt.

1843.   Nicolls, F. H. G., late Capt. 4th Dragoon Gds.

1841.   Nicolls, Robert M., late Capt. 65th Regiment

1860.   Nightingale, Arthur C., Capt. 93rd Highlanders

1854.   Nisbit, Thomas, Major 1st Dragoon Guards

1854.   Nixon, Arthur James, Major Rifle Brigade

1847.   Noad, Arthur M., Lieutenant Royal Navy

1856.   Noel, Charles P., late Lieutenant 48th Regt.

1846.   Noel, Hon. G. J., *M.P.*, late Capt. 11th Hussars

1845.   Noel Hon. H. L., late Lieut. 68th Lt. Infantry

1851.   Norbury, T. C., late Capt. 6th Dragoon Guards

1853.   Norcliffe, Norcliffe, *K.H.*, Major-General

O.M.   Norcott, William S. R., *C.B.*, Col. unattached

1858.   Norris, William, Captain Rifle Brigade

1852.   Norman, Charles J. W., Major 72nd Highlanders

1847.   Norman, Henry R., Lieut.-Col. 10th Regiment

1853.   Northcote, L. Stafford, late Captain 39th Regt.

1857.   Norton, Chas. G. Campbell, Capt. 23rd Fusiliers

1859.   Nugent, Andrew, Captain 2nd Dragoons

1840.   Nugent, James, Lieut.-Col. 36th Regiment

1846.   Nugent, St. George M., Major unattached

1859.   Nunn, J. L. W., Captain 80th Regiment

O.

1846.	Oakes, Thomas G. A., Lt.-Colonel 12th Lancers
1841.	O'Brien, Bartholomew, Lt.-Colonel Mil. Train
1843.	O'Callaghan, C. C., late Captain 1st Drg. Gds.
1846.	O'Callaghan, H. D., late Capt. 32nd Regiment
1849.	O'Callaghan, J, late Captain 62nd Regiment
1842.	O'Conor, Rich. J. R., Major 17th Regiment
1838.	Ogle, Graham, Captain Royal Navy
1840.	O'Grady, Hon. T. G., Major, late 74th High.
1853.	O'Hara, James, late Capt. 2nd Dragoon Guards
1859.	O'Hara, Richard, Captain Royal Artillery
O.M.	O'Keefe, James, Paymaster half-pay 48th Regt.
O.M.	O'Leary, Arthur, Major, late 55th Regiment
1852.	Oliver, George C., Lieutenant Royal Navy
1841.	Oliver, Richard Aldworth, Captain Royal Navy
1858.	Oliver, Thomas W., Lieutenant Royal Navy
1858.	O'Malley, W. B., late Lieut. 25th Regiment
1850.	Orde, John W. P., late Capt. 42nd Highlanders
1846.	Orme, William H., Major 85th Light Infantry
1840.	Orme, William K., Lt.-Colonel 10th Regiment
1839.	Ormsby, Anthony, Major unattached
1842.	Ormsby, John W., Colonel Royal Artillery
1838.	Ormsby, Thomas, late Capt. 92nd Highlanders

1839.   Otway, Arthur J., late Lieutenant 2nd Regiment
O.M.   Otway, C., Major-Gen. ret. full-pay R. Artillery
1839.   Ouvry, Henry Aime, *C.B.*, Lt.-Col. unattached
1858.   Owen, Arthur R., Lieutenant Royal Navy
1838.   Owen, Charles Cunliffe, Captain Royal Navy
1840.   Owen, H. C. C., *C.B.*, Lt.-Col. R. Engineers

P.

1852. Paget, Richard H., Captain 66th Regiment
1851. Pakenham, Hon. F. B., Major unattached
1844. Pakenham, T. H., Lt.-Colonel 30th Regiment
1859. Palliser, John A., Lieutenant 76th Regiment
1858. Palliser, W. R. G., Commander Royal Navy
1846. Palmer, Arthur W., late Captain 5th Fusiliers
1852. Palmer, Frederick, Captain Scots Fus. Guards
1851. Palmer, Francis R., *C.B.*, Lt.-Col. 60th Rifles
1858. Palmer, Henry W., Captain 74th Highlanders
1851. Parish, John E., Commander Royal Navy
1855. Park, William Ker, Surgeon 16th Lancers
1856. Parke, R., Lt.-Col. Royal Marines Lt. Infantry
1848. Parke, William, *C.B.*, Colonel 53rd Regiment
1846. Parker, Arthur C., Major 71st Highlanders
1853. Parker, George, Captain Royal Navy
1841. Parkinson, C. A., late Captain 37th Regiment
1858. Parr, Robert A., Lieutenant Royal Navy
1854. Parratt, E. L., late Captain 85th Lt. Infantry
1853. Parry, Legh R., Captain and Adj. Depôt Batt.
1857. Parry, Richard, late Cornet 2nd Dragoons
1843. Parry, W., Deputy Inspector General half-pay
1851. Pasley, George M., Captain Royal Artillery

1842.	Paterson, Augustus, late Capt. 41st Regiment
1851.	Paterson, F. T. L., Captain 63rd Regiment
1840.	Paterson, P. H., late Ensign 92nd Highlanders
1855.	Paton, James, Captain 4th Regiment
1839.	Paton, John, late Lieutenant 91st Regiment
1854.	Patterson, Charles J., Captain 35th Regiment
1840.	Patterson, W. T. L., Lt.-Col. 91st Regiment
1858.	Patterson, W., Captain and Adj. R. M. College
O.M.	Pattle, Thomas, Colonel 1st Dragoon Guards
1855.	Patton, Henry B., Captain 27th Regiment
1844.	Patton, W. D. P., Colonel 74th Highlanders
1855.	Paulet, C. William, Captain 9th Lancers
1847.	Payn, William, *C.B.*, Lt-Col. 72nd Highlanders
1856.	Payne, Henry L., Lieut. 2nd Dragoon Guards
1838.	Payne, William R., Lieutenant Royal Navy
1851.	Paynter, George, Major, late 1st Dragoon Grds.
1860.	Peach, H. Peach K., Capt. Royal Horse Grds.
1843.	Peach, J. P., Major, late 1st Dragoon Guards
1846.	Peacocke, George J., Lieut.-Col. 16th Regiment
1845.	Peacocke, W. W. R., Lieut. half-pay 17th Regt.
1852.	Peareth, William, late Capt. 4th Light Dragoons
1850.	Pearson, R. L. Otway, Major Grenadier Gds.
1851.	Pearson, Samuel, late Lieut. 1st Dragoon Gds.
1859.	Pearson, William Charles, Captain 88th Regt.
1840.	Peat, David, Captain Royal Navy
1847.	Pedder, Charles D., Captain 39th Regiment
1858.	Peel, Arthur Lennox, Major 52nd Regiment

1845. Peel, Edmund Yates, Lieut.-Colonel unattached
1852. Peel, John, Major H.P. Depôt Battalion
1852. Peel, Robert M., late Captain 6th Dragoons
1855. Peel, W. Henry, late Captain 9th Regiment
1853. Pelly, Raymond R., Captain 37th Regiment
1858. Pelly, Henry R., Captain Royal Engineers
1855. Pemberton, W. Leigh, Captain 60th Rifles
1846. Pennington, C. P., late Lieut. Rifle Brigade
1858. Pennington, Hon. J. F., late Capt. Rifle Brigade
1847. Penrice, Herbert N., late Capt. Royal Engineers
1858. Penton, Thomas, Major 8th Hussars
1857. Pepys, Edmund, late Lieutenant 1st Dragoons
1854. Perceval, Charles G. G., late Lieut. Royal Navy
1857. Percival, Philip, Captain 79th Highlanders
1838. Percy, A. C. Heber-, late Lieut. Rifle Brigade
1848. Percy, John William, Captain 9th Regiment
1856. Pering, George H., Captain 18th Hussars
1858. Perry, John L., Commander Royal Navy
1853. Persse, Dudley, late Captain 7th Fusiliers
1852. Persse, Walter B., late Captain 22nd Regiment
1860. Persse, William N., Lieutenant Royal Artillery
O.M. Perston, D., *M.D.*, Surg. H.P. 13th Lt. Drgs.
O.M. Petrie, S., *C.B.*, late Director of the Commissariat
1847. Peyton, Francis, Lieut.-Colonel 98th Regiment
1853. Phelips, H. P., Captain Royal Artillery
1844. Phelips, Richard, late Captain Royal Artillery
1851. Phelips, William D., late Captain 60th Rifles

1858. Philips, Edward W., Captain 36th Regiment
1860. Philips, N. Geo., late Captain 47th Regiment
1851. Philipps, George, late Captain 23rd Fusiliers
1849. Phillimore, William B., late Capt. Gren. Gds.
1858. Phillipps, John James, Captain 60th Rifles
1860. Phillipps, Paul W., Captain Royal Artillery
1844. Phillips, R. Newton, Colonel Depôt Batt. Chatham
O.M. Phillpotts, A. T., Colonel Royal Artillery
1841. Phipps, H. B., late Captain 31st Regiment
1856. Phipps, P. A. L., late Captain 29th Regiment
1847. Pierce, Frederick, late Captain 96th Regiment
1839. Pigott, Arthur, Lt.-Col. H.P. 20th Regiment
1855. Pigott, Henry De R., Captain 83rd Regiment
1853. Pigott, John Pelling, Major unattached
1847. Pigou, Arthur C., Captain Royal Artillery
1841. Pilgrim, Charles, late Cornet 2nd Dragoons
1846. Pilgrim, John Bunce, Captain unattached
1850. Pilleau, Henry, Staff-Surgeon-Major
1856. Pinckney, Philip, late Capt. 6th Dragoon Grds.
1849. Pipon, J. K., Colonel Assis. Adj.-Gen. Horse Gds.
O.M. Pipon, Manaton, late Capt. 1st Dragoon Guards
1852. Pipon, Philip G., Major Royal Artillery
1848. Pitcairn, Andrew, Major depôt Battalion
1843. Pitman, Edmund, late Captain 55th Regiment
1840. Pitt, W. G., late Lieutenant 11th Hussars
1858. Pitt, T. H., Captain Royal Artillery
1854. Platt, Fred. W., late Ensign 95th Regiment

1848.   Platt, T. E. H., late Lieutenant 49th Regiment

1841.   Plunkett, Hon. E. S., Major late 95th Regiment

1856.   Pocklington, G. Henry, Captain 18th Regiment

1849.   Pole, Cecil C., late Lieut. 90th Light Infantry

1853.   Pole, Edward, Colonel 12th Lancers

1845.   Pole, Samuel, Major, late 12th Lancers

1856.   Ponsonby, Hon. Ashley, late Capt. Gren. Gds.

1853.   Ponsonby, Arthur E. V., Capt. Grenadier Gds.

1847.   Porcher, Edwin A., Lieutenant Royal Navy

1846.   Portal, Robert, Major 5th Lancers

1854.   Porter, Henry R., Captain Royal Artillery

1854.   Porter, John, Lieut.-Colonel 67th Regiment

1838.   Porter, Thomas, Captain Royal Navy

1847.   Poulett, William H., late Capt. 22nd Regiment

1858.   Powell, Francis G., Captain 2nd Dragoon Gds.

O.M.   Powell, Thomas F., late Captain 16th Lancers

1844.   Powell, W. Martin, late Captain 6th Dragoosn

O.M.   Power, Kingsmill M., late Capt. 16th Lancers

1847.   Pownall, Walter, Major 3rd Buffs

1853.   Pratt, W. C., late Captain 67th Regiment

1859.   Prendergrast, Lenox, Captain 2nd Dragoons

1853.   Prentis, William T., late Captain 2nd Dragoons

1855.   Preston, Charles E., Capt. & Paymstr. 18th Regt.

1858.   Preston, I. N., late Captain 3rd Light Dragoons

1849.   Preston, Richard, Major 44th Regiment

1838.   Prettejohn, R. B., Lt.-Col. 14th Light Dragoons

1855.   Pretyman, Arthur C., late Capt. 25th Regiment

1852.	Pretyman, William, Lieut.-Col. late 60th Rifles
1848.	Prevost, T. W., Capt. H.P. 42nd Highlanders
O.M.	Priaulx, H.S.G., late Lieut. 4th Light Dragoons
1854.	Priaulx, Oswald De L., Captain 94th Regiment
1839.	Price, Edward, *C.B.*, Colonel Royal Artillery
1855.	Price, George B., Captain 2nd Dragoons
1846.	Price, R. Blackwood, Lt.-Colonel H.P. R. Artil.
1846.	Price, Robert H., Major 35th Regiment
1842.	Prime, Arthur, late Capt. 5th Dragoon Guards
1855.	Prince, William S., late Capt. 71st Highlanders
1846.	Pringle, J. H., Colonel, late Scots Fusilier Gds.
1855.	Probyn, Edmund, late Lieutenant 6th Dragoons
1841.	Prothero, E., late Captain 14th Regiment
1842.	Pryce, J. E. H., late Captain 2nd Regiment
O.M.	Pryse, Edward L., *M.P.*, late Captain 3rd Buffs
1855.	Puget, Granville, W., Captain 34th Regiment
1856.	Puget, John, Captain 8th Hussars
1853.	Purcell, P. V., late Captain 13th Light Dragoons
1858.	Puxley, J. L., late Captain 6th Dragoons
1855.	Pyper, Rev. R., late Asst.-Surgeon 11th Hussars

Q.

1851. Queade, William H., Captain 12th Regiment
1856. Quicke, Sidney G., Major 53rd Regiment
1851. Quin, Hon. W. W., late Captain Grenadier Gds.

R.

1844. Radcliffe, William P., Lt.-Colonel 20th Regt.
1850. Rae, James A., late Lieutenant 27th Regiment
1844. Ramsay, B. D. W., Major unattached
1846. Ramsay, James, Colonel unattached
1842. Ramsay, R. W., late Captain 42nd Highlanders
1853. Ramsay, William F., late Lieut. 54th Regiment
1843. Randolph, C. Wilson, Lt.-Colonel Grenadier Gds.
1855. Rattray, James C., Captain 90th Light Infantry
1858. Rawlinson, William S., Captain 6th Dragoons
1843. Read, B. M., late Lieutenant 15th Hussars
O.M. Read, Edward R., late Captain 12th Regiment
1840. Reed, William, late Captain 6th Regiment

1860. Redmond, John Patrick, Major 61st Regiment

O.M. Reignolds, T. S., *C.B.*, Maj.-Gen. ret. full-pay

1850. Reilly, Hugh A., Commander Royal Navy

1850. Reilly, W. E. M., *C.B.*, Major Royal Artillery

1860. Rendall, J. K., late Captain 5th Lancers

1858. Rennie, Geo., Dep.-Assist. Commissary.-Gen.

1850. Renny, Henry, Captain Royal Artillery

1847. Renton, A. C. C., Major, late 42nd Highlanders

1853. Retallack, Francis, Captain 63rd Regiment

O.M. Reynolds, Charles W., late Captain 16th Lancers

O.M. Reynolds, J. W., Lieutenant-Colonel, Deputy
Adjutant-General to Forces in Jamaica

1854. Rhodes, Frederick, late Captain 98th Regiment

1848. Rhodes, Godfrey, Major unattached

1853. Rice, Cecil, Major 72nd Highlanders

1858. Rich, Charles David, Major 9th Lancers

O.M. Rich, Sir C. H. J., Bt., late Cornet 14th Lt. Drgs.

1853. Rich, G. W. T., Lt.-Colonel 71st Highlanders

1846. Richards, William, late Captain 17th Lancers

1849. Rickford, T. P., late Captain 23rd Fusiliers,
(Exon of the Yeomen of the Guard)

1851. Rickman, William, Major Depôt Battalion

1843. Riddell, T. M., late Lieut. 7th Dragoon Guards

1838. Ridley, John H. E., late Lieut. 2nd Drg. Gds.

1848. Rigaud, Gibbes, Major 60th Rifles

1847. Rising, Benjamin, late Lieut. 76th Regiment

H

1851.   Roberts, Bertie M., late Capt. 26th Regiment
1842.   Robertson, Andrew, late Captain 87th Fusiliers
1854.   Robertson, A. M., Captain 4th Dragoon Guards
1858.   Robertson, G. Metcalf, Captain 1st Dragoons
1855.   Robertson, Henry J., late Captain Rifle Brigade
1847.   Robertson, J., *M.D.*, Surg. H.P. 13th Regt.
1840.   Robertson, James E., Lt.-Colonel 6th Regiment
1842.   Robertson, J. H. C., Lt.-Col. H.P. 100th Regt.
1847.   Robertson, J. P., *C.B.*, Lt.-Colonel Mil. Train
1847.   Robertson, P., *M.D.*, Staff-Surgeon half-pay
1854.   Robinson, H. J., late Lieutenant 76th Regiment
1858.   Robinson, H. K., late Lieutenant 4th Regiment
1848.   Robinson, R. Harcourt, Captain 60th Rifles
1841.   Robyns, Thomas, late Captain 32nd Regiment
1860.   Rochfort, C. G., Captain 20th Regiment
1852.   Rocke, James H., Capt., & Adjt. Depôt Battalion
1845.   Rodney, George B., Major R. Marines Lt. Infy.
1841.   Rodney, M. H., Commander Royal Navy
1841.   Rodney, T. M., Commander Royal Navy
1848.   Roe, Peter Burton, Lieut.-Colonel 60th Rifles
1840.   Roe, P. F., late Lieutenant 60th Rifles
1858.   Roe, Robert E., Lieutenant 12th Lancers
O.M.   Rofe, Saml., Major & Paym. H.P. 14th Lt. Drgs.
1847.   Rogers, H., Major Royal Artillery
1842.   Rogers, Henry D., *C.B.*, Captain Royal Navy
1852.   Rogers, J. F., Assistant Commissary-General

1859. Rogers, John T., late Captain 33rd Regiment
1840. Rolland, S. E., late Lieutenant 69th Regiment
1858. Rolleston, Cornelius C., Major 84th Regiment
1838. Rolls, Alexander, late Lieut. 4th Dragoon Gds.
1843. Romer, Robert W., Major 59th Regiment
1842. Rooper, B., late Lieutenant 34th Regiment
1851. Rooper, H. G., late Capt. 85th Light Infantry
1848. Ross, Albert Ernest, Captain 5th Fusiliers
1850. Ross, G. W., late Lieutenant 92nd Highlanders
1848. Ross, John, Lieutenant-Colonel Rifle Brigade
1846. Ross, Robert L., Lt.-Col. 93rd Highlanders
1840. Ross, Thomas, Lieut.-Colonel 73rd Regiment
1848. Rosser, George F., Major & Paym. 16th Lancers
1857. Rotton, Charles P., Captain Royal Artillery
1858. Rous, William J., Capt. Scots Fusilier Guards
1849. Rowland, George, Captain 1st Royals
1850. Rowland, W. H., Captain 55th Regiment
1842. Rowles, Henry, late Lieutenant 8th Hussars
1849. Rowles, James, late Captain Rifle Brigade
1846. Rowley, Hon. H. L., late Capt. 6th Dragoons
1838. Rush, Alfred, late Captain 77th Regiment
1839. Russell, Lord A. G., Lt.-Colonel Rifle Brigade
1838. Russell, Lord C. G., Maj., late 93rd Highlanders
1852. Russell, R., late Lieutenant 2nd Regiment
1841. Russell, Sir W., Bart., *C.B.*, Lt.-Col. 7th Hussars
O.M. Ruxton, John H. H., late Lieut. 4th Regiment

1852. Ruxton, William F., Lieutenant Royal Navy
1850. Ryan, George A., Major 70th Regiment
1854. Ryan, Valentine, Captain 64th Regiment

S

1860.	St. Clair, Archibald, Lieutenant Royal Navy
1855.	St. Clair, C. William, Major 57th Regiment
1856.	St. George, Howard, late Lieut. 77th Regiment
1848.	St. George, T. C. B., Captain 78th Highlanders
1851.	St. John, Frederick A., Captain unattached
1849.	St. John, John Henry, Major 92nd Highlanders
1856.	St. John, St. A. B., Lieutenant 10th Regiment
1839.	St. Leger, John, Major, late 14th Lt. Dragoons
1842.	Salmon, William P., late Captain 60th Rifles
1856.	Saltmarshe, Arthur, Captain 70th Regiment
1848.	Saltmarshe, P., late Lieutenant 8th Hussars
1841.	Saltoun, Alexander, Lord, Major, late 28th Regt.
1851.	Salwey, Alfred, Assistant-Commissary-General
O.M.	Sanders. Frederick P., late Capt. 43rd Lt. Inf.
1846.	Sanders, Robert, *C.B.*, Colonel late 32nd Regt.
1842.	Sandes, W. S., late Captain 11th Hussars
1840.	Sandilands, Hon. James, late Capt. 8th Hussars
1850.	Sarel, Henry A., Major 17th Lancers
1853.	Sargent, John Neptune, Lieut.-Col. 3rd Buffs
1851.	Sartoris, A., late Captain 7th Hussars
1850.	Saumarez, Thomas, Captain Royal Navy
1848.	Saunders, E., late Cornet 2nd Dragoon Guards

1858. Saunders, George R., late Captain Rifle Brigade
1847. Saunders, W. B., Captain Royal Horse Artillery
1848. Savage, Frederick S., Major 68th Light Infantry
1857. Savage, F. W., late Lieut. 13th Light Dragoons
1838. Savile, Henry B. O., Capt. H.P. Royal Artillery
1839. Sawyer, Charles, Lt.-Colonel 6th Dragoon Gds.
1853. Sayer, Frederic, Captain H.P. 23rd Fusiliers
1846. Sayer, Jas. R. S., Lt.-Col. 1st Dragoon Guards
1858. Scheberras, Attilio, Captain 98th Regiment
1848. Scobell, H. S., late Captain 2nd Dragoons
1838. Scott, Alfred, Major late 1st Dragoon Guards
1858. Scott, Arthur, Major 5th Fusiliers
1852. Scott, Beresford, Paymaster Royal Navy
1855. Scott, Edward, Major late 8th Hussars
O.M. Scott, George F. C., Col. 76th Regt. ret. full-pay
1858. Scott, Henry, Major 18th Hussars
1853. Scott, John B., Lieutenant Royal Navy
1850. Scott, James Robt., late Capt. 4th Dragoon Gds.
O.M. Scott. John S., late Captain 31st Regiment
1842. Scott, W., late Captain 6th Dragoon Guards
1850. Scott, William, late Captain 79th Highlanders
1858. Scott, Lord Walter C., late Captain 15th Hussars
1841. Scudamore, A., *C.B.*, Lt.-Col. 14th Lt. Dragoons
1860. Seagrave, O'Neil, Captain unattached
1847. Segrave, William F., Captain 71st Highlanders
1851. Serocold, Walter P., late Captain 66th Regiment
1852. Servantes, W. F. G., Dep.-Assis.-Comy.-Gen.

1853.	Severne, John Edmond, late Capt. 16th Lancers
1849.	Sewell, Algernon R., Major 15th Regiment
1846.	Seymour, C. H., late Captain 85th Regiment
1841.	Seymour, H. R., late Captain 40th Regiment
1850.	Seymour, Wm. H., *C.B.*, Lt.-Col. 2nd Drg. Gds.
1856.	Seymour, William H., late Lieut. 7th Hussars
1841.	Shadwell, C. F. A., *C.B.*, Captain Royal Navy
1850.	Shadwell, Lawrence, Lieut.-Colonel unattached
1859.	Shakerley, G. S., Captain Royal Artillery
1860.	Sheffield, John C., Captain 21st Regiment
1852.	Sheldon, E. R. C., late Captain 63rd Regiment
1848.	Shelley, Edward, late Captain 16th Lancers
1854.	Sheppard, Thomas, Captain 4th Regiment
O.M.	Sherson, Alex. N., late Capt. 72nd Highlanders
1849.	Sherston, J. D., late Capt. 6th Dragoon Guards
1853.	Shipley, Conway, late Lieutenant Royal Navy
1849.	Shirley, Walter D., late Lieut. 50th Regiment
1839.	Shute, Charles C., Colonel 6th Dragoons
1844.	Shute, Neville Hill, Lt.-Colonel 64th Regiment
1849.	Shute, William G., Captain 28th Regiment
1859.	Shute, Henry Douglas, Captain 57th Regiment
1846.	Sibthorp, C. C. W., late Captain 1st Dragoons
1846.	Sibthorp, R. F. W., Lieut.-Colonel unattached
1855.	Sidebottom, Leonard, Capt. & Adj. Dépôt Batt.
1858.	Sidney, Henry M., Captain 1st Dragoon Gds.
1851.	Simpson, W. H. R., Major Royal Artillery
1853.	Singleton, E. Cecil, late Capt. 51st Lt. Infantry

O.M.   Singleton, John, Major-General

1857.   Sitwell, Frederick, late Capt. 3rd Lt. Dragoons

O.M.   Skey, J., *M.D.*, Inspector-General of Hospitals

O.M.   Skinner, T., Major, late Ceylon Rifle Regiment

1849.   Skipwith, Sidmouth S., Commander Royal Navy

1842.   Skurray, Francis C., Major 24th Regiment

1859.   Slade, Alfred F. A., Captain 100th Regiment

1843.   Slade, Herbert D., Major 1st Dragoon Guards

1858.   Slade, Henry, Surgeon Royal Navy

1848.   Slade, William H., Major 5th Lancers

1854.   Sleeman, Henry A., late Lieut. 16th Lancers

1852.   Smart, Henry Hawley, Captain 17th Regt.

1846.   Smith, Charles H., Lt.-Col. Royal Artillery

1858.   Smith. Charles F., Captain 71st Highlanders

1856.   Smith, Fitzroy G., Major 7th Dragoon Guards

1845.   Smith, Hugh, Lieutenant-Colonel unattached

1856.   Smith, H. H.. *M.D.*. Surgeon Royal Navy

1845.   Smith, J. L., Major-Gen. Royal Art. ret. full pay

1854.   Smith, Michael E., Captain unattached

1840.   Smith, M.M., late Captain 92nd Highlanders

1850.   Smith, Percy S., late Capt. 13th Lt. Dragoons

1851.   Smith, Richard P., Major late 10th Hussars

1848.   Smith, Richard S., Commander Royal Navy

1838.   Smith, S. Lionel, Major, late 54th Regiment

1846.   Smith, Thomas, *C.B.*, Lt.-Col. 90th Lt. Infantry

1839.   Smith, T. Chaloner, late Lieut. 11th Hussars

1848.   Smyth, Edward S., Colonel unattached

1858. Smyth, E. Skeffington R., late Lieut. 28th Regt.
O.M. Smyth, Henry, *C.B.*, Colonel 76th Regiment
1858. Smyth, Ralph, late Captain 17th Regiment
1850. Snow, Arthur H. C., Captain 96th Regiment
1855. Snow, Edmund B., Captain R. Marines Lt. Inf.
1848. Somerset, A. P. F. C., late Lieut. 13th Lt. Inf
1847. Somerset, P. G. H., *C.B.*, Lt.-Col. 7th Fusiliers
1841. Sotheby, C. W. H., late Captain 60th Rifles
1860. Sotheby, Fred. Edwd., Captain Rifle Brigade
1838. Sparkling, Charles, late Captain 15th Hussars
O.M. Sparks, J. P., *C.B.*, Colonel 38th Regiment
1838. Spicer, John W. G., late Capt. 3rd Drg. Gds.
1849. Spicer, R. William, late Captain 16th Lancers
1847. Spring, Robert, late Captain 21st Fusiliers
1850. Spurway, John, Major Royal Artillery
1848. Stacey, Edward, late Captain 18th Hussars
1853. Stack, Frederick R., Captain 65th Regiment
1858. Standish, W. S. Carr, late Lieut. 7th Hussars
1847. Stanhope, Chandos S. S., Captain Royal Navy
1850. Stanhope, R. C., late Lieut. 13th Lt. Infantry
1842. Stanley, J. Talbot, late Captain 89th Regiment
1852. Stapleton, F. G., Captain Grenadier Guards
1845. Stapylton, G. G. C., Lt.-Col. 32nd Regiment
1853. Stapylton, H. M., Major 2nd Dragoon Guards
1843. Staunton, George, Colonel Cape Mounted Rifles
1859. Steel, Charles, Major unattached

1850. Steele, Augustus F., Lt.-Col. 9th Lancers
1855. Stephens, Adolphus H., Captain Rifle Brigade
1858. Stephens, Richard, late Captain 60th Rifles
1847. Stephens, W., late Lieutenant 64th Regiment
1860. Stephenson, S. Vane, Capt. Scots Fus. Gds.
1839. Sterling, Sir A. C. *K.C.B.*, Col. unattached
1852. Steuart, David, Captain 34th Regiment
1838. Stevenson, G. R.. late Lieut. 7th Dragoon Gds.
1851. Stevenson, H. H., Major unattached
1852. Steward, Edwin A. T., Major 21st Fusiliers
1853. Steward, Edward H., late Captain 60th Rifles
1848. Steward, F. G., Captain late unattached
1858. Steward, Henry H., Captain 2nd Dragoon Gds.
1845. Steward, Richard O. F., Major unattached
1852. Stewart, A., *M.D.*, Inspec.-Gen. of Hospitals
1860. Stewart, Hon. R. R., Lieut. 42nd Regiment
1846. Stewart, John H., Captain R. Marines Lt. Inf.
1842. Stewart-Mackenzie, W., late Lieut. 90th Lt. Inf.
1858. Stewart, Robert Crosse, Major 35th Regiment
1839. Stewart, Thomas D., Captain Royal Navy
1853. Stewart, W. G. D., Major unattached
1855. Stirling, C. Edward, Captain Royal Artillery
1853. Stirling, John S., Captain Royal Artillery
1853. Stisted, H. W., *C.B.*, Colonel 93rd Highlanders
1848. Stisted, Thomas H., Major 7th Hussars
1857. Story, John B., late Lieutenant Rifle Brigade
1840. Story, R. W., Colonel ret. full-pay R. Artillery

1840.	Strathmore, T.G., Earl of, late Lieut. 1st Life Gds.
1858.	Strange, Charles J., Major Royal Artillery
1851.	Stratton, John, late Lieutenant 38th Regiment
1850.	Street, J. A., *C.B.*, Colonel Depôt Battalion
1855.	Strickland, Walter, Commander Royal Navy
1850.	Stringer, Miles, late Lieutenant 6th Dragoons
1848.	Stronge, M. Du Prè, late Capt. 52nd Lt. Infantry
1855.	Stroud, Henry W., Captain 63rd Regiment
O.M.	Stuart, George F., late Captain 49th Regiment
1850.	Stuart, Hon. James, Major Rifle Brigade
1845.	Stuart, J. S. S., late Capt. 1st Dragoon Guards
1855.	Stuart, Robert C. W., late Captain 2nd Regt.
1855.	Stuart, W. Edington, Captain 15th Hussars
1844.	Studdert, C. Fitz-Gerald, Maj. late 80th Regt.
1842.	Suckling, Robert W., Commander Royal Navy
1857.	Sullivan, Francis W., Commander Royal Navy
1859.	Sullivan, George, Captain 80th Regiment
1858.	Sunter, Thomas M., *M.B.*, Staff Surgeon
1842.	Surtees, Charles F., late Capt. 3rd Lt. Dragoons
1838.	Surtees, Henry E., late Lieutenant 10th Hussars
1849.	Sutherland, Francis, late Capt. 2nd Dragoons
1845.	Sutton, Charles, late Captain 12th Lancers
1846.	Sutton, Francis, late Captain R. Horse Guards
1839.	Sutton, Frederick, late Captain 11th Hussars
1844.	Sutton, H. George, late Lieut. 12th Lancers
1859.	Swaby, George, late Captain Military Train
1851.	Swaffield, Charles J. O., Major 31st Regiment

O.M.   Swan, Graves C., Colonel, late unattached

1860.   Swann, Jno. T., Lieutenant Royal Navy

1853.   Swinburne, James, Capt. 3rd Dragoon Guards

1849.   Swinburne, Thomas A., Lieutenant Royal Navy

1855.   Swindley, John E., Captain 6th Dragoons

1851.   Swinfen, F. H., Captain 5th Dragoon Guards

1842.   Swinny, George S., Captain 15th Hussars

1853.   Sykes, Cam., Major late 80th Regiment

1844.   Sykes, Frederick, late Captain 11th Hussars

1843.   Sykes, Sir F.W., Bart., late Lieut. 2nd Life Gds.

1846.   Sykes, Joseph A., late Captain 94th Regiment

T.

1849. Talbot, Hon. W. L., Major unattached
1843. Tarn, John, Surgeon Royal Navy
1847. Taswell, Edward, Captain Royal Artillery
1856. Tattnall, A. H., late Captain 92nd Highlanders
1851. Tattnall, Robert C., Commander Royal Navy
1849. Taylor, G. Cavendish, late Lieut. 95th Regiment
1844. Taylor, H. Cavendish, late Lieut. 17th Lancers
O.M.   Taylor, R. C. H., *C.B.*, Col. H.P. Depôt Batt.
1858. Taylor, Robert K., Lieutenant 85th Regiment
1848. Taylor, R. M., late Lieutenant 25th Regiment
1856. Taylor, Wm. O'B, Captain 18th Regiment
1854. Teesdale, C. C., *C.B.*, *V.C.*, Major Royal Art.
1852. Teesdale, Charles P., Captain 11th Regiment
1858. Temple, Edwyn F., Captain 55th Regiment
1855. Temple, Grenville M., Lieutenant Royal Navy
1851. Temple, John, Lieut.-Colonel, late 60th Rifles
1858. Tewart, John Edward, Captain 6th Regiment
1848. Thellusson, A. D., Lt.-Col., late 72nd Highlanders
1848. Thellusson, C. S., late Captain 12th Lancers
1858. Thesiger, Hon. C. W., Captain 6th Dragoons
1850. Thistlethwayte, A. F., late Ensign 26th Regt.

1850. Thomas, Barclay, Major 27th Regiment
1860. Thomas, Freeman, late Lieut. Rifle Brigade
1847. Thomas, H. J., Lt.-Colonel H.P. Royal Artillery
1845. Thomas, J. Wellesley, Lt.-Colonel 67th Regt.
1855. Thomas, Lloyd H., Captain 91st Regiment
O.M. Thomas, Morgan, Inspector-Gen. of Hospitals
1849. Thompson, Arnold, Lt.-Col. Royal Artillery
1860. Thompson, Alfred, late Cornet 1st Dragoons
1848. Thompson, C. W., Lt.-Colonel 7th Drg. Gds.
1853. Thompson, Daniel, Captain 67th Regiment
O.M. Thompson, Frederick, late Capt. 6th Dragoons
1854. Thompson, John, Captain 2nd Regiment
1843. Thompson, P. S., Lt.-Col. 14th Light Dragoons
1851. Thompson, Richard, Major unattached
1846. Thomson, A. S., *M.D.*, Staff-Surgeon-Major
1838. Thomson, J. A., late Captain 13th Lt. Dragoons
1854. Thomson, Robert C., Captain 2nd Regiment
1850. Thomson, R. T., Major 1st Dragoon Guards
1855. Thornhill, Henry, Captain Royal Artillery
1854. Thornhill, W. C. C., late Capt. 23rd Fusiliers
1846. Thoroton, Thomas, late Captain 1st Dragoons
1858. Thorp, Edward Buller, Major 89th Regiment
1838. Thorp, William, Commander Royal Navy
O.M. Thurlow, Hon. J. E. H., late Capt. 85th Lt. Inf.
O.M. Thurlow, Hon. T. H. H., late Capt. 7th Fusiliers
1850. Thursby, J. H., late Lieut. 90th Light Infantry
1854. Thursby, James L., Captain 22nd Regiment

1850.	Thursby, R. L., Captain Cape Mounted Rifles
1838.	Tibbits, J. Borlase, late Captain 12th Lancers
1846.	Tighe, F. E., late Captain 82nd Regiment
1854.	Tillbrook, Philip L., Captain 50th Regiment
1850.	Timins, O. F. F., late Captain 82nd Regiment
1858.	Timson, Henry, late Captain 5th Lancers
1848.	Tinling, Wm. P., Lt.-Col. 90th Light Infantry
1856.	Tod, R. A. Boothby, Captain 94th Regiment
1845.	Todd, J. Augustus, Lt.-Col. 14th Lt. Dragoons
1856.	Todd, J. A. Ruddell, Captain 87th Fusiliers
1856.	Tom, Daniel, late Captain 89th Regiment
1849.	Tomkinson, E., Major Cavalry Depôt, Canterbury
1848.	Tomlin, B., late Captain 1st Dragoon Guards
1844.	Tonge, Louis C. H., Commander Royal Navy
1850.	Tongue, Vincent, Captain 60th Rifles
1850.	Tower, Conyers, Captain 3rd Dragoon Guards
1848.	Townsend, H. S., late Lieut 2nd Life Guards
1855.	Travers, Francis S., Captain 60th Rifles
1853.	Travers, James D., Captain 17th Regiment
1855.	Travers, J. O., Lt.-Colonel R. Marines Lt. Inf.
1851.	Travers, Richard H., Captain 24th Regiment
1841.	Travers, R. O., late Capt. 1st Dragoon Guards
1859.	Tredcroft, C. Lennox, Captain Royal Artillery
1846.	Tredcroft, Edm., late Lieut. 4th Lt. Dragoons
1854.	Trelawny, H. D., late Captain R. Horse Guards
1850.	Trelawny, H. R. S., late Lieut. 6th Dragoons
1848.	Tremayne, Arthur, Lt.-Col. 13th Lt. Dragoons

1846. Trench, P. Le Poer, Lt.-Col., late 2nd Drg. Gds.

1855. Trevelyan, H. Astley, Major 7th Hussars

1853. Tritton, G. Sinclair, late Lieut. 7th Fusiliers

1838. Troubridge, Sir T. St. V., Bart., *C.B.*, Colonel, Deputy Adjutant-General

1852. Trousdell, W.G., *M.D.*, Surgeon 13th Regt.

1841. Trower, Frederick C., Capt., late 4th Regiment

1842. Trower, Horace, Captain 15th Hussars

O.M. Trueman, Charles J., late Lieut. 6th Drg. Gds.

1851. Tryon, Thomas, Major 7th Fusiliers

1860. Tryon, George, Commander Royal Navy

1850. Tuite, Joseph, late Lieutenant 15th Regiment

1852. Tuite, Thos. B., Captain 11th Regiment

1843. Tulloch, Thomas, Lt.-Col. late 1st Drg. Gds.

1849. Tunstall, A., late Captain 1st W. I. Regiment

1839. Tupper, Charles W., late Lieut. 7th Fusiliers

1852. Tupper, Daniel W., Major 50th Regiment

1856. Tupper, De Vic, Captain 8th Regiment

1855. Tupper, G. Le M., Major Royal Horse Artillery

1844. Turner, F. C, Polhill, late Capt. 6th Drg. Gds.

1859. Turner, Henry Scott, Lieut. 69th Regiment

1847. Turner, Mansfield, late Captain 20th Regiment

1855. Turner, Nath. O. S., Lt.-Col. Royal Artillery

1847. Turton, E. H., late Captain 3rd Dragoon Gds.

1843. Tuthill, William, late Capt. 1st Dragoon Gds.

1844. Tweeddale, John D., Surgeon Royal Navy

1859. Twemlow, W. H., Lieut. 27th Regiment

1858.   Twynam, Philip A. A., Captain 15th Regt.
1855.   Tyler, Henry W., Captain Royal Engineers

U.

1858. Uniacke, Charles H., Captain 2nd Dragoons
1852. Uniacke, Henry T., late Captain 19th Regt.
1857. Upton, Edward, J., Captain 26th Regiment
1855. Urquhart, J., Capt. Paymaster 27th Regiment
1854. Urquhart, Wm. H., Captain 75th Regiment
1848. Ussher, Sidney H., Captain Royal Navy

V.

1840. Valiant, Thomas J., Major-General, ret. full-pay
1858. Vane, F. Fletcher, Major 23rd Fusiliers
1849. Vance, Horatio P., Major 38th Regiment
1859. Vanderspar, W. Chas., Major Ceylon R. Regt.
1856. Vansittart, C. R., late Captain 11th Hussars
1850. Vansittart, Edward W., Captain Royal Navy
1853. Vansittart, F., late Lieut. 14th Light Dragoons
1844. Vansittart, Francis, Capt. H.P. Royal Artillery
1855. Vardon, Noel H. B., Captain 13th Lt. Infantry
1856. Vaughan, E. C., Captain Royal Artillery
1860. Vaughan, G. A., Captain 1st West I. Regiment
1855. Venables, Cavendish, late Capt. 74th Highlanders
1849. Venables, Thomas, Captain 97th Regiment
1855. Vernon, Charles E. H., Commander Royal Navy
1851. Vernon, R. V. D., late Lieutenant 60th Rifles
1854. Vesey, Chas. C. W., Captain 72nd Highlanders
1843. Vialls, George C., Lieut.-Colonel 95th Regiment
1839. Vialls, Henry T., Major late 45th Regiment
1855. Vibart, James M. C., Captain Royal Artillery
1852. Vivian, J. E., late Lieut. 13th Light Dragoons
1858. Voss, Howell W., Surgeon Royal Artillery
1852. Vyse, Edward H., Captain 3rd Light Dragoons

W.

1852. Waddilove, Charles L., Commander Royal Navy
1838. Waddington, Henry S., late Capt. Rifle Brigade
O.M. Wade, George, late Captain 13th Light Infantry
1853. Wade, James H., Major 53rd Regiment
1858. Wadman, Arthur J. P., Capt. 1st Drg. Guards
1850. Walcott, Charles E., Major Royal Artillery
1845. Wale, Robert G., late Captain 33rd Regiment
1838. Walhouse, Edward, late Captain 12th Regiment
1841. Walker, C. P. B., Colonel 2nd Dragoon Guards
1860. Walker, Edwyn, Captain 15th Hussars
1854. Walker, Sir G., Bart., late Capt. Coldstream Gds.
1859. Walker, G. A. A., Captain Royal Artillery
1848. Walker, Hercules, Major Rifle Brigade
1855. Walker, Henry T., Major 25th Regiment
1858. Walker, J. W., late Lieut. 7th Dragoon Guards
1855. Walker, William F., Captain Royal Artillery
1858. Wall, Thomas Fred., Surgeon 38th Regiment
1846. Wallack, Henry J., late Captain 77th Regiment
1854. Waller, William N., Captain Royal Artillery
1849. Wallington, John W., late Capt. 4th Light Drgs.
1860. Walrond, Charles W., Lieut. Royal Artillery
1843. Walshe, H. C., *M.D.*, Surgeon Royal Artillery

1843. Walter, Edward, late Captain 8th Hussars
1853. Walter, Frederick A., Major 97th Regiment
1850. Walters, Henry, late Lieutenant 6th Dragoons
1850. Warburton, Augustus F., late Capt. 15th Regt.
1858. Warburton, G. A., late Captain 19th Regiment
1856. Ward, Bernard Edward, Major 60th Rifles
1842. Ward, Edward, W., Captain Royal Engineers
1849. Ward, M. F., late Lieut. 90th Light Infantry
1841. Ward, T. H., late Captain 85th Light Infantry
1858. Ward, Hon. W. J., Commander Royal Navy
1854. Warde, George, Captain 51st Light Infantry
1846. Waring, Francis Robert, Surgeon-Major
1848. Warre, Arthur B., Lieutenant Royal Navy
1838. Warre, Henry J., *C.B.*, Colonel 57th Regiment
1850. Warren, Arthur F., Major Rifle Brigade
1854. Warren, Henry Edward, Captain 60th Rifles
O.M. Warren, William S., late Captain Rifle Brigade
1839. Warriner, Erule, late Captain 16th Lancers
O.M. Warner, R., late Captain 3rd Dragoon Guards
1852. Warry, William, Major Depôt Battalion
1859. Watts-Russell, D. G. N., Captain 60th Rifles
1858. Watson, Sir C., Bart., late Lieut. 71st Highanders
1854. Watson, George W., Commander Royal Navy
O.M. Watson, Sir J., *K.C.B.*, General, Col. 14th Regt.
1853. Watson, W., Lt.-Colonel late 3rd Lt. Dragoons
1855. Watson, W. John P., late Captain 17th Lancers

1842. Way, G. Lewis, Major, late 29th Regiment
1848. Webb, J. M., late Captain 4th Dragoon Guards
1852. Webb, Robert W., late Lieut. 37th Regiment
1859. Webb, Stph. M., *M.D.*, Assist.-Surg. 36th Regt.
1848. Webb, W. F., late Lieutenant 17th Lancers
1846. Webster, Sir A. F., Bart., Lieut. Royal Navy
1859. Webster, Guy, Lieutenant 16th Lancers
1853. Webster, James, late Lieut. 79th Highlanders
1839. Wedderburn, J. K., late Captain 10th Hussars
1841. Wedderburne, Charles F., late Capt. 53rd Regt.
O.M. Weguelin, Thos. M. L., Lieut.-Col. unattached
1850. Weir, John Charles, Captain 2nd Regiment
1855. Wells, Richard, Lieutenant Royal Navy
1846. Wemyss, D. D., late Lieutenant 48th Regiment
1854. Wemyss, J. O., Capain 3rd Buffs
1850. West, Frederick, Major Depôt Battalion
1841. West, James B., Commander Royal Navy
O.M. Western, Thomas H., late Capt. 15th Regiment
1856. Westhead, G. E. Brown, Major Depôt Battalion
1843. Westmacott, Spencer, Lt.-Colonel R. Engineers
1845. Westmoreland, Francis Earl of, *C.B.*, Colonel,
        late Coldstream Guards
1860. Wetherall, J. P., Captain 6th Dragoons
1853. Weyland, R. H., late Captain 43rd Regiment
1854. Wheatstone, J. B., Lt.-Col. 8th Regt. ret. full-pay
1858. Wheatley, Wm., Lt.-Col., late Scots Fus. Gds.
1849. Whitby, T. E., late Capt. 3rd Dragoon Guards

1856.   White, Augustus B., Captain 15th Regiment

1858.   White, Alfred H., Lieut. 3rd Dragoon Guards

1855.   White, Edward, Lieutenant Royal Navy

1853.   White, Henry, Captain 13th Light Dragoons

1848.   White, Luke, late Captain 13th Light Dragoons

1842.   White, M., *M.D.*, Staff-Surgeon 1st Class, H.P.

1841.   White, P., Surgeon half-pay 72nd Highlanders

1854.   White, Robert, Lieut.-Colonel 17th Lancers

1851.   White, R. H., Lt.-Colonel Scots Fusilier Gds.

1842.   White, Thomas, Lt.-Colonel, late 49th Regiment

1848.   White, Thomas W., Major 16th Lancers

1843.   Whitehead, F. J. G., late Capt. 42nd Highlanders

1855.   Whitehead, William, Captain 80th Regiment

O.M.   Whitfeild, Henry W., Colonel 2nd W. I. Regt.

1856.   Whitmore, G. S., Major 62nd Regiment

1858.   Whitshed, James H., Lieutenant Royal Navy

O.M.   Whittingham, F., *C.B.*, Colonel 4th Regiment

1839.   Whittingham, Paul B., Lt.-Col. R. Engineers

1850.   Whittingstall, Geo. F., late Capt. 12th Lancers

1838.   Whitty, Irwin S., late Captain 8th Regiment

1851.   Wickham, Edward T., Major 61st Regiment

1843.   Wigsell, A. D., late Capt. 2nd Dragoon Gds.

1844.   Wilbraham, T. E., late Captain 39th Regiment

1841.   Wilby, William, Lieut.-Colonel 4th Regiment

1854.   Wildbore, Fred., late Assist.-Surg. Colds. Gds.

1859.   Wildman, L., Commander Royal Navy

1838.   Wilkie, John, Colonel unattached

1855. Wilkin, Henry J., Lieutenant 7th Hussars
1858. Wilkinson, A. E., Captain 7th Hussars
1856. Wilkinson, F. G., Lt.-Colonel 42nd Highlanders
1849. Wilkinson, George A., Captain Royal Artillery
1850. Wilkinson, Johnson, Captain 15th Regiment
1849. Wilkinson, James A., late Capt. 15th Regimen
1856. Willan, S. L. D., Captain 2nd Regiment
1846. Willan, Wm. M. D., Capt. H.P. Royal Artillery
1845. Willett, J. Saltren, late Capt. Royal Artillery
1838. Williams, A. Wellesley, Captain Millitary Train
1852. Williams, Edward A., Major Royal Artillery
1852. Williams, G. L., late Captain 24th Regiment
1849. Williams, Henry F., Major 60th Rifles
1846. Williams, J. Penry, late Ensign 1st Royals
1854. Williams, R. M., Major 3rd Light Dragoons
1858. Williams, Reginald S., Capt. 93rd Highlanders
1854. Williams, T., late Lieutenant 10th Hussars
1845. Williams, T. Bigoe, late Capt. 4th Dragoon Gds.
O.M. Williams, Walter, late Captain 17th Lancers
O.M. Williams, Sir W. F., Bart., *K.C.B.*, Major-
         General Royal Artillery
1850. Williams, W.W. R., late Lieut. 4th Dragoon Gds.
1855. Williamson, Aug. H., late Capt. 30th Regiment
1854. Williamson, Charles, Captain 60th Rifles
1851. Williamson, G., *M.D* , Staff-Surgeon 2nd Class
1854. Williamson, William, Major 85th Light Infantry
1859. Willis, Charles W., Captain 33rd Regiment

1857. Willis, Frederick A., *C.B.*, Lt.-Col. 38th Regt.
1858. Willis, Sherlock V., Captain 1st Royals
1855. Willoughby, H. S., Captain 45th Regiment
1858. Wilmot, Henry, *V.C.*, Major Rifle Brigade
1844. Wilson, Chas. Townsend, Lt.-Col. late Colds. Gds.
1838. Wilson, F. T. H., late Lieutenant 8th Hussars
1846. Wilson-Atkinson, G.C., late Captain 7th Fusiliers
1860. Wilson, J. E. M., Lieutenant Royal Navy
1849. Wilson, M. W., late Cornet 11th Hussars
1860. Wilson-Tod, W. H., late Captain 39th Regiment
O.M. Wilson, Thomas M., Colonel 8th Regiment
1852. Wilson, Willoughby J., Capt. Royal Artillery
1856. Windham, George S., Captain Rifle Brigade
1853. Wing, Vincent, Major Depôt Battalion
O.M. Wingate, T., late Captain 2nd Regiment
1858. Wingfield, C. G., late Lieut. 71st Highlanders
1839. Wingfield, John H., Lt.-Colonel 15th Regiment
1854. Wingfield, W. C., Captain 1st Dragoon Guards
1854. Winn, E. W., late Lieutenant Royal Artillery
1845. Winthrop, Geo. T. S., Commander Royal Navy
1841. Winthrop, H. E. S., Commander Royal Navy
1854. Wirgman, Theodore, Major unattached
1852. Woddrop, W. Allen, late Lieut. 2nd Dragoons
1846. Wodehouse, Edmund, Lt.-Colonel 24th Regt.
1858. Wolseley, Garnet J., Lt.-Col. 90th Lt. Infantry
1860. Woodgate, Francis, Lieut. 2nd Life Guards
1858. Wombwell, Adolphus U., Capt. 12th Lancers

1847. Wombwell, Arthur, Major Depôt Battalion

1840. Wood, E. R., late Lieutenant 12th Lancers

1856. Wood, Henry, Captain 91st Regiment

1855. Wood, James J., Captain 45th Regiment

O.M. Wood, L. E., Major retired full-pay 54th Regt.

1854. Wood, William, Commander Royal Navy

1848. Wood, W. S., late Lieut. 7th Dragoon Guards

1847. Woodley. Augustus J., Commander Royal Navy

1840. Woulfes, R., late Lieutenant 7th Fusiliers

1858. Wright, Charles, Captain Royal Artillery

1838. Wright, John G., late Lieut. 30th Regiment

1854. Wright, Thos., late Lieut. 3rd Dragoon Guards

O.M. Wright, Thomas D., late Lieut. 89th Regiment

1846. Wrottesley, Hon. G., Captain Royal Engineers

1859. Wroughton, H. A. C., Lieut. 13th Regiment

1851. Wyatt, Charles E., Captain 5th Lancers

1856. Wyatt, John, Surgeon Coldstream Guards

1839. Wyke, Sir Chas. J., *K.C.B.*, late Lieut. 7th Fus.

1846. Wyndowe, W.F., Staff-Adjutant London District

1841. Wynn. H.W.W.,*M.P.*,Lt,-Col. late 2ndW.I.R.

Y.

1844.   Yard, Frederick, Major, late 17th Regiment

1838.   Yates, E. R. W. W., Lt.-Colonel unattached

1855.   Yates, Henry Peel, Lt.-Col. Royal H. Artillery

1860.   Yeo, Gerard, *M.D.*, Staff-Surgeon Royal Navy

O.M.   Yonge, G. N. K. A., Major Depôt Battalion

1857.   Yonge, Henry, J., Captain 61st Regiment

1846.   Yonge, W. J., Lt.-Col. 60th Rifles, ret. full pay

1857.   Yonge, William L., Captain Royal Artillery

1838.   Yorke, James C., late Capt. 5th Dragoon Guards

1846.   Yorke, T. Y. Dallas, late Capt. 11th Hussars

1858.   Young, Edward W., *M.D.*, Surgeon 60th Rifles

1853.   Young, George S., Major 80th Regiment

1853.   Young, G. R. C., Captain Royal Artillery

1853.   Young, Horatio B., Captain Royal Navy

1852.   Young, J. B., late Captain 51st Light Infantry

1849.   Young, Thomas, Captain 22nd Regiment

1838.   Young, W. Pym, Lieut.-Colonel 65th Regiment

This List is corrected to 1st January, 1861.

THOMAS WALCOT, Secretary.

HONORARY MEMBERS.

COLONEL

HIS ROYAL HIGHNESS

THE PRINCE OF WALES, *K.G.*

HIS IMPERIAL MAJESTY,

NAPOLEON III.

EMPEROR OF THE FRENCH

HIS ROYAL HIGHNESS

PRINCE ADALBERT OF PRUSSIA.

Henry F. Downes, Esq.
George Bentinck Lefroy, Esq., *Solicitor.*
Charles O. Parnell, Esq., . *Architect.* .
Thomas Walcot, Esq., . *Secretary.*

HONORARY VISITOR.

Alfred Smith, Esq., . . . *Architect.*

PICTURES, BUSTS, MAPS, SCULPTURE, &c.

PRESENTED BY

NAPOLEON III., Emperor of the French.
Piece of Gobelin Tapestry, 1784. *Staircase.*

ABBOTT, George, Esq.,
Bust of Field-Marshal the late Lord Raglan, *G.C.B.*
Staircase.

BEAUFORT, Sir Francis.
Chart of the North-West Passage, discovered by Captain
McClure, H.M.S. "*Investigator.*" *Library.*
Charts of the Baltic and Black Seas, 2 vols., folio. *Ditto.*

CLARKE, T. J., Captain Royal Navy.
Bombardment of Algiers, 27th August, 1816.
Visitors' Dining Room.

COLSTON, E., Esq., late 15th Hussars.
(Engravings.)
Portrait of Field Marshal Lord Raglan, *G.C.B.* } *Visitors'*
Portrait of the late Duke of Beaufort } *Drawing*
"A Dialogue at Waterloo." } *Room.*
"None but the brave deserve the fair." } *Smoking Room.*
"Highland Nurses." }
Meeting of the Royal Hounds on Ascot
Heath.
Beaufort Hunt. } *Card Room.*
Meet at Melton.
Quorn Hunt.

DANIELL, H., Colonel late Coldstream Guards.

Fruit Piece. *House Dining Room.*

Portrait of His Royal Highness the late Duke of Cambridge (Lithograph.) *Visitors' Drawing Room.*

Bust of His Royal Highness the Duke of Cambridge. *Entrance Hall.*

Bust of Napoleon III., Emperor of the French. *Visitors' Drawing Room.*

} By Jones.

Portrait of Napoleon III, Emperor of the French, (Lithograph.) *Visitors' Drawing Room.*

Portrait of Major-General Sir Henry Torrens, *K.C.B.* (Engraving.) *Secretary's Room.*

Colossal Bust of Field-Marshal the Duke of Wellington, by Behnes. *Inner Hall.*

DURHAM, The late Admiral Sir Philip

full-length Portrait of himself. *Staircase.*

DURANT, G. C., late Captain 12th Lancers.

Equestrian Statuette of the Emperor Napoleon III. (in Bronze.) *Evening Room.*

HALE, J. R. Bladgen, Colonel Unattached.

Statuettes (in Ivory) of

Field-Marshal the Duke of Wellington, and

The Emperor Napoleon I. *Visitors' Drawing Room.*

HISLOP, Lady.

Arrowsmith's Map of India. *Vestibule.*

HOSEASON. J., Captain Royal Navy.

Two Chromo-Lithographs, "Peace and War," shewing Bourne's New System of Indian River Navigation. *3rd Billiard Room.*

JERVOIS, E. S., Captain H.P. 7th Fusiliers.

Sevastopol, from the Malakoff, after the Siege. (Coloured Lithograph.) *Card Room.*

KING, H. B., Captain Royal Navy.

Six Views of the Baltic, during the late Russian War.

Library.

LEES, G. C., Esq., late 61st Regiment.

Assembling for the Waterloo Banquet at Apsley House. (Engraving.) *Card Room.*

MANNING, J. S., late Captain 1st Dragoon Guards.

Battle of Camperdown. *Visitors' Dining Room.*

Full-length Portraits (in one Picture) of the Marquis of Anglesey, and the late Vice-Admiral Sir Charles Paget.

Writing Room.

Clock and Marble Case on centre Chimney Piece. } *Coffee Room.*

Two Silver Snuff Boxes.

MEMBER, A.

Two Coloured Lithographs—" Woman's Mission," " Works of Mercy."

Card Room.

PACK, A. J. Reynell, *C.B.*, Colonel H.P. 7th Fusiliers.

Portrait of the late Major-General Sir Denis Pack, *K.C.B.* (Engraving.) *Writing Room.*

PANMURE, Right Hon. Lord.

Selection of Crimean Maps and Lithographs. *Library.*

POLE, Samuel, Major, late 12th Lancers.

Marble Bust of Lord Nelson. *Evening Room.*

Map of London in the Reign of Queen Elizabeth.

Vestibule.

ROWLAND, G. T., Colonel retired full pay Royal Artillery.

Napoleon at Fontainbleu, (Proof.)

Visitors' Drawing Room.

Portrait of the Great Duke of Marlborough.

Visitors' Dining Room.

STUART, G. F., late Captain 49th Regiment.
    The Chelsea Pensioners.   *Smoking Room.*
WASHINGTON, Capt., R. N., F.R.S.
    Charts.   *Library.*
WHEATLEY, William, Lt.-Col. late Scots Fusilier Guards.
    Ordnance Map, of the Country 50 miles round London,
    (inch scale.)   *Writing Room.*
WILLIAMS, J. Penry, Esq., late 1st Royals.
    Miniature Portrait of Lady Hamilton.   *Writing Room.*

ABSTRACT OF THE ACCOUNTS

OF THE

ARMY AND NAVY CLUB,

From the 1st January to the 31st December, 1859.

ARMY AND NAVY CLUB.

REPORT OF THE COMMITTEE OF MANAGEMENT,
27TH APRIL, 1860.

The Committee of Management, in accordance with the Regulations of the Club, have the honor to lay before the Members an Abstract of the Accounts, ending 31st December, 1859, duly examined and certified by a Public Accountant, with an Estimate of the Probable Receipts and Expenditure for the current year.

The excess of Receipts over Expenditure during the past year amounted to £2,761 19s. 2d., and was applied to the payment of the sum drawn prospectively on the Receipts of 1859, and £1,600 on the amount similarly advanced in liquidation of the Mortgage of £3,000 originally granted to Mrs. Justice.

The Committee beg to draw attention to the following statements, exhibiting the result of the financial operations since the completion and opening of the New House, and showing the present effective strength of the Club, both of which they trust will be deemed satisfactory.

In 1851 the Debt was	£85,928	13	9	The Annual Interest	£3,890	1	0
In 1860	74,150	0	0	Ditto ditto	3,200	0	0
Diminution of Debt	£11,778	13	9	Diminution of Interest Annually ...	£690	1	0

Total number of Members paid Annual Subscriptions for 1859 ... 1990
    Of whom during the Year Died   27
    Retired   40
    Placed on Supernumerary List 142
                                               209
          Leaving Effective Members, ... 1781

The Actual Vacancies during the Year 1859, have been—
    Died at Home and Abroad   ... 44
    Retired   ditto   ditto   41
                        85

Upon which number the Entrances in the Estimate for 1860 has been framed.

It will be observed by the Estimates for the current year, that Provision to the amount of £600 has been made, for the formation of a reserve fund, to meet the periodical requirements of the Property. The Committee trust the foregoing arrangement will prevent any future addition to the Club's liabilities, to diminish which, they purpose appropriating any remaining surplus of Receipts over Expenditure.

                    H. I. DANIELL,
                        Late Coldstream Guards,
                              CHAIRMAN.

RECEIPTS.

	£	s.	d.	£	s.	d.
1 Entrance Sub., elected 1855, 30*l.*	30	0	0			
1 „ „ „ 1856, 30*l.*	30	0	0			
1 „ „ „ 1857, 30*l.*	30	0	0			
44 „ „ „ 1858, 30*l.*	1,320	0	0			
91 „ „ „ 1859, 30*l.*	2,730	0	0			
				4,140	0	0
138 Entrances						
1808 Annual Subscrips. 1859 ..6*l.* 6*s.*	11,390	8	0			
182 returned from Supernu-						
merary .. .. 6*l.* 6*s.*	1,146	12	0			
				12,537	0	0
1990						
5 Arrears Subscrips. 1858 ..6*l.* 6*s.*	31	10	0			
4 Fines .. each 2*l.* 0*s.*	8	0	0			
				39	10	0
2575 Library Subscriptions .. 5*s.*	..	..		643	15	0
				17,360	5	0
Interest on Deposit Account, Union						
Bank	21	2	6			
Ditto, Current Account ditto ..	50	6	10			
Deductions on Tradesmen's Accounts	74	18	9			
				146	8	1
Receipts for Billiards	275	14	0			
„ for Baths	48	4	6			
„ for Shoe Cleaner ..	10	19	11			
Rent of Drawers, Mezzanine Floor..	4	0	0			
				338	18	5
Received for Cards	529	13	9			
Paid for ditto	387	0	6			
				142	13	3
Received for Cigars	1,292	5	2			
Paid for ditto	1,152	14	2			
				139	11	0
Received for Wines	5,264	2	0			
Paid for ditto	4,595	10	8			
				668	11	4
Received for Spirits, Ales, &c...	1,934	15	0			
Paid for ditto..	1,700	8	7			
				234	6	5
Carried forward ..	..	..		19,030	13	6

EXPENDITURE.

	£ s. d.	£ s. d.
Drawn on account of 1858 and paid 1859	.. ..	1,127 7 6
Additions to Stock. Furniture	92 15 0	
Plate	216 8 0	
Plated	21 10 0	
Cutlery	28 17 0	
Linen	62 12 9	
		422 2 9
New Carpet in Coffee Room ..	.. ..	234 0 0
Interest on Debentures, one year .. £3,261 18 0		
Dividend to Mrs. Justice, 8 months 91 19 1		
	3,353 17 1	
Rates and Taxes. Assessed Taxes, 4 Quarters .. 167 12 6		
Parochial Rates, 4 Quarters .. 235 10 8		
Land Tax, 2 Houses in Pall Mall .. 21 18 0		
St. James's Sq. Rate . 4 7 0		
Water Rate, 4 Qrs. .. 52 10 0		
Property Tax, 4 Qrs. .. 112 10 0		
General and Sewers Rate.. .. 132 10 0		
	726 18 2	
Insurance on House, Furniture, and Plate Glass	136 4 0	
Salaries—Secretary .. 350 0 0		
Ditto for fulfilling the duties of Treasurer on the resignation of Mr. Charles Downes . 50 0 0		
Addition to Salary in 1851, on completion of the New House, confirmed by Gen. Meet. 100 0 0		
Assistant to Secretary.. 60 0 0		
Wages. Steward .. 160 0 0		
Butler 100 0 0		
Steward's dept. (47) 1,260 16 5		
Butler's „ (3) 73 0 0		
Housekpr's. „ (14) 299 17 8		
Kitchen „ (15) 517 18 4		
	2,971 12 5	
Carried forward	7,188 11 8	1,783 10 3

RECEIPTS.—*Continued.*	£	s.	d.	£	s.	d.
Brought forward	..	..		19,030	13	6
1 new Debenture issued £160, at £6 11 0 per annum ..	160	0	0			
1 old Debenture cancelled £135, at £6 11 0 per annum	135	0	0			
				25	0	0

NOTE—Surplus on the Receipts and Expenditure, 1859 £2,761 19 2
Paid on account of 1858 ..£1,127 7 6
Mrs. Justice's Mortgage..1,600 0 0
           2,727 7 6

Balance carried forward 34 11 8

| Carried forward .. .. .. | .. | .. | | 19,055 | 13 | 6 |

EXPENDITURE.—*Continued.*				£ s. d.	£ s. d.
Brought forward	..		..	7,188 11 8	1,783 10 3
Extra Attendance	..	127 11	9		
Liveries and Hats		579 13	0		
				707 4 9	
Expended for Provisions	..	11,848 8	6		
Received in Coffee Room	..	9,480 5	8		
Difference carried to Board of Servants, averaging 10s. 9½d. per week each Servant			..	2,368 2 10	
Fuel. Coals	..	514 11	0		
Coke	.. ..	16 16	0		
Charcoal ..	..	119 6	0		
Gas for Cooking		40 10	9		
Spirits of Wine	..	11 10	0		
Wood..	..	37 14	0		
				740 7 9	
Lghtng. Lamp Oil, Glasses, &c.		149 10	0		
Wax and Tallow	..	32 0	0		
Gas ..	..	741 19	3		
				923 9 3	
Stationery and Account Books			..	263 17 11	
Newspapers, English	..	297 1	2		
„ Foreign		23 11	4		
		320 12	6		
Deduct sold second-hand		74 1	6		
				246 11 0	
Printing and Advertising		82 15	6		
Ditto New List of Members		44 17	0		
				127 12 6	
Washing House Linen			..	430 0 0	
Repairs to Furniture Upholstery & General Repairs	..	73 9	0		
New Venetian Blinds		8 8	0		
Cleaning and Calenlendering Blinds	..	12 19	6		
Cleaning and Repairing Chandeliers and Lamps	..	10 9	6		
Drugget and Felt		16 3	0		
				121 9 0	
Carried forward	.. ..		..	13,117 6 8	1,783 10 3

RECEIPTS.—*Continued.*	£	*s.*	*d.*
Brought forward	19,055	13	6
Carried forward	19,055	13	6

EXPENDITURE.—*Continued.*	£	s.	d.	£	s.	d.
Brought forward	13,117	6	8	1,783	10	3

Repairs to House, &c.

Ironmongery, Pipes, and Stoves 68*l.* 11*s.*; New Bath Steam Boiler 30*l.* 16*s.*; Plumber's Work 24*l.* 1*s.* Painting and Glazing 7*l.* 3*s.* 11*d.*; Drains and Bricklayer 14*l.* 13*s.*; Mason and Repairing Stone Work 17*l.* 1*s.*; Cleaning Marble Chimney Pieces 8*l.* 10*s.*; Polishing Scagliola 17*l.* 11*s.*; Carpenter's Work 44*l.* 12*s.*; Alterations 9*l.*; French Polishing 9*l.* 13*s.*; Ventilators 2*l.* 5*s.*; Gas Fittings and Repairs 23*l.* 14*s.*; Contract for Keeping Water Closets in order, 12 months 20*l.* .. .. — **297 10 11**

	£	s.	d.			
Whitewashing, Cleaning, and Dusting House throughout	74	14	0			
Taking up, Beating, and Re-laying Carpets	14	13	0			
		89	7	0		
Repairs to and keeping Billiard Tables in order, Tubes, &c. ..		52	0	6		
Repairs to Kitchen Utensils, Tinning ditto by contract, Repairs and Winding Clocks by contract, Ice Machines, &c.		121	0	9		
Soap & articles for cleaning	103	5	0			
Sweeping Chimnies by contract, 12 months ..	12	0	0			
		115	5	0		
Turnery, Brushes, Mats, Baskets, &c.		99	9	0		
Ice, Foreign and Rough		320	8	0		
Illuminations—Her Majesty's Birthday		35	8	0		

Miscellaneous—including Snuff 13*l.* 3*s.* 6*d.*; Subscription to St. George's Hospital, 5*l.* 5*s.*; Medical Attendance for Servants, 20*l.*; Toothpicks, 17*l.* 4*s.* 6*d.*; Sand, 18*l.* 1*s.*;

| Carried forward .. .. | 14,247 | 15 | 10 | 1,783 | 10 | 3 |

RECEIPTS.—*Continued.*	£	s.	d.
Brought forward	19,055	13	6
Total	19,055	13	6

EXPENDITURE.—*Continued.*	£	s.	d.	£	s.	d.
Brought forward	14,247	15	10	1,783	10	3
Cleaning Skylights and Ornamental Glass, 21*l.* 1*s.* 6*d.*; Cleaning Bude and Sun Lights, 27*l.* 16*s.*; Small Hand Paper, 30*l.* 4*s.*; Kitchen Pans and Earthenware, 35*l.* 1*s.*; Engraving and Repairing Glass, 18*l.* 12*s.* 2*d.*; Postages, Receipt and Postage Stamps, 22*l.* 6*s.* 7*d.*; Allowance for Breakages, 150*l.*; Rick Cloth for Skylight, 8*l.* 18*s.*; Gratuities, 33*l.*; Skeleton Device for Illumination, 25*l.* 17*s.*; Sundries, 76*l.* 16*s.* 8*d.*	523	6	11			
				14,771	2	9
Completing China and Glass Stock	..	..		196	17	0
Pension to W. Keeble, 12 months	..	..		20	0	0
Racing Telegraph Intelligence, 12 months	..	..		25	0	0
New Iron Bins to Wine Cellar ..	..	..		57	3	0
New Illumination Devices ..	..	..		154	0	0
Legal Expenses, 1858-59	..	..		19	12	0
Accountant Auditing Accounts for 1858	..	..		21	0	0
Library. { New Books	120	12	10			
Maps and Charts ..	19	11	0			
Periodicals, Magazines, &c. ..	104	7	0			
Subscriptions to Circulating Library	37	10	0			
New Reading Desk	10	15	0			
Librarian, (in addition to his Salary as Assistant to Secretary	40	0	0			
Book Binding	40	1	0			
				372	16	10
Paid off on Account of the Mortgage to Mrs. Justice	..	..		1,600	0	0
				17,893	14	4
Balance of Cash in hand, 31st December, 1859.	..	..		34	11	8
				19,055	13	6

Due to Members of the Club—	£	s.	d.	£	s.	d.
Original issue of Debentures ..						
571 Debentures, at £135	77,085	0	0			
Cancelled						
1853, 126 ,,						
1854, 11 ,,						
1855, 17 ,,						
1856, 28 ,,						
1857, 2 ,,						
1858, 17 ,,						
1859, 1 ,,						
202	27,270	0	0			
Leaving 369 Old Debentures at £135	..	..		49,815	0	0
Issued New Debentures,						
1853, 106						
1854, 4						
1855, 9						
1856, 7						
1857, 2						
1859, 1						
129 at £160	..	..		20,640	0	0
Amount of debt on which Interest is paid, 498 Debentures ..	..	..		70,455	0	0
Advanced from Current Account, *not bearing Interest, vide* statement on the opposite side.						
17 Debentures, at £135 each	2,295	0	0			
Ditto ditto balance of Mrs. Justice's Mortgage	1,400	0	0			
				3,695	0	0
Total Amount of Debt, 31st Dec.	..	..		74,150	0	0
Estimated balance of Property in favor of the Club.	..	..		50,548	5	6
				124,698	5	6

	£	s.	d.	£	s.	d.
Original Purchase of Freehold Ground and Expenses	..	..		51,395	14	8
New House, valued 31st Dec., 1858	54,629	6	0			
Additions, 1859	354	13	11			
	54,983	19	11			
Deduct Wear and Tear, 2 per cent.	1,099	13	1			
				53,884	6	10
Furniture valued 31st Dec., 1858	8,279	2	0			
Additions and Repairs, 1859	458	19	0			
	8,738	1	0			
Deduct Wear and Tear 12 months, 10 per cent.	873	16	0			
				7,864	5	0
Plate Glass Mirrors	..	..		656	0	0
Plate, ⎰Plate and Plated Goods	1,976	10	0			
Linen, ⎱Linen	798	13	0			
&c. ⎱Cutlery, China and Glass ..	1,135	9	0			
				3,910	12	0
Library.⎰Books and Maps, 31st December, 1858 ..	3,308	5	10			
⎱Purchased & Bound, 1859	160	13	10			
				3,468	19	8
Cellar⎰Wines on hand	932	3	6			
⎰Liqueurs, Spirits, &c. ..	71	10	0			
⎱Sodas, Ales, &c.	13	15	6			
				1,017	9	0
Cigars—Stock on hand, at cost price	..	..		166	6	8
Her Majesty's Portrait, Pictures, Tapestry, &c., (sum insured thereon)	..	..		2,300	0	0
Cash at Union Bank, 31st Dec. 1859	1,861	14	10			
Advanced for Wines, &c., per account of 1860..	1,863	0	11			
Advanced on account of Debentures of £135 cancelled, to be re-issued in new Debentures of £160 each, in lieu thereof	2,295	0	0			
Balance of Mrs. Justice's Mortgage	1,400	0	0			
In the hands of the Steward, &c. ..	240	0	0			
	7,659	15	9			
Liabilities due 31st December, 1859, paid 1860	7,625	4	1			
				34	11	8
				124,698	5	6

REPORT

On examining the Accounts of the Army & Navy Club for the year 1859.

ADDRESSED TO THE COMMITTEE.

I certify that I have verified the entries in the Cash Book, by the Receipts and Payments in the Banker's Pass Book, and I have examined the Postings of the Cash Book into the Ledger, and checked all the additions.

I have also compared the Payments for the year 1859 with the Vouchers for the same, and have inspected the Vouchers for the payment of the Liabilities at the close of the year, amounting to £7,625 : 4 : 1, the whole of which amount has been since paid off.

I have further examined the General Abstract of Receipts and Payments for the year 1859, and the Valuation of Assets, and have found the same correct, and I may be permitted to testify to the extremely able and accurate manner in which the Accounts of the Club have been kept by the Secretary.

(Signed)   **ALFRED B. ENGLISH,**

ACCOUNTANT,

26th April, 1860.

18, Lincoln's Inn Fields.

RECEIVED.	£	s.	d.	£	s.	d.
Entrance Subscriptions	4,140	0	0			
Annual Subscriptions, Miscellaneous, &c.	14,915	13	6			
				19,055	13	6

EXPENDED.	£	s.	d.	£	s.	d.
Additions to, and Renovation of Furniture, Plate, Linen, &c... ..	656	2	9			
Interest on Debentures, &c. ..	3,353	17	1			
Ordinary Repairs to House ..	386	17	11			
Extraordinary Repairs to House	57	3	0			
Ordinary Repairs to Furniture ..	121	9	0			
Extraordinary Expenditure ..	..	..				
Incidental Expenditure	..	..				
Establishment, Current Expenses, &c.	11,718	4	7			
				16,293	14	4
Surplus of Receipts over Expenditure during the year	..	..		2,761	19	2
				19,055	13	6

RECEIPTS.		£	s.	d.	£	s.	d.
85 Entrance Subscriptions £30	0	0	2,550	0	0		
1800 Annual Subscriptions 6	6	0	11,340	0	0		
100 from Supernumerary 6	6	0	630	0	0		
2500 Library Subscriptions 0	5	0	625	0	0		
						15,145	0	0
Interest on Monies Invested ..			200	0	0		
Miscellaneous Receipts ..			1,300	0	0		
						1,500	0	0

H. I. DANIELL,

Chairman.

16,645	0	0

from 1st January to the 31st December, 1860.

EXPENDITURE.	£	s.	d.	£	s.	d.
Additions to Furniture, Plate and Linen	400	0	0			
Library Books and Binding ..	500	0	0			
				900	0	0
Interest on Debentures	3,200	0	0			
Rates, Taxes, and Insurance ..	800	0	0			
Establishment	5.950	0	0			
Coals, Charcoal, Coke, and Wood	730	0	0			
Lamp Oil, Candles, and Gas ..	920	0	0			
Newspapers, English and Foreign	250	0	0			
Stationery, Account Books, and Printing	350	0	0			
Washing House Linen ..	430	0	0			
Furniture and House Repairs						
Tinning and Repairing Kitchen Utensils	590	0	0			
Billiard Tables, &c.						
Extraordinary Repairs to Kitchen	165	0	0			
Miscellaneous	950	0	0			
				14,385	0	0
				15,285	0	0
Reserved Fund for Septennial Repairs, New Carpets, &c. ..	..		..	600	0	0
Probable Balance on the ordinary Receipts over Expenditure during the Year 1860.	..		..	760	0	0
				16,645	0	0

CPSIA information can be obtained at www.ICGtesting.com
Printed in the USA
BVOW01s1207080714

358479BV00022B/826/P